Praise for
The Three Condi...

"Moshe Gersht turns spiritual truths into medicine our hearts are longing for."

MARIANNE WILLIAMSON
New York Times bestselling author

"Gersht embodies the idea that if you're happy, you're helping cocreate a better world, and living with that reminder is an immeasurable gift. The personal insight in the book provides readers with a kind and sturdy friend to lean on."

SHARON SALZBERG
New York Times bestselling author of *Lovingkindness* and *Real Life*

"*The Three Conditions* offers valuable insights and practical wisdom for anyone seeking personal growth and transformation. It reminds us that we have the ability to overcome fear, embrace change, and live in alignment with our authentic selves. I highly recommend this book to those who are ready to awaken their inner power and create a lasting impact in their lives."

GREG MCKEOWN
podcaster, *New York Times* bestselling author of
Effortless and *Essentialism*

"This book is a welcome addition to the canon of works on intention by someone who has personally experienced the full power of thoughts to create the life you are living—for better or worse. Follow Moshe Gersht's own journey, and pick up a load of invaluable nuggets on how to awaken your latent power and transform your life."

LYNNE MCTAGGART
international bestselling author of *The Field*,
The Intention Experiment, and *The Power of Eight*

"This book contains living Torah within its pages, and I can only imagine how much it will help the masses, especially those searching for their path to connect with God."

RAV ASHER WEISS
author of *The Minchas Asher*

"Moshe paints an inspiring and clear path to living with more love, joy, and peace every day!"

DAVID MELTZER
speaker, author, entrepreneur, host of
The Playbook with David Meltzer podcast

"There is wisdom on every page of this guide to how to live a purpose-filled, meaningful life. A mixture of scholarly research and life lessons learned the hard way, *The Three Conditions* offers a shortcut to enlightenment, but you won't want to rush through the priceless nuggets that Moshe so expertly shares."

SUZANNE GIESEMANN
author of *Messages of Hope*

"I appreciate and admire Moshe Gersht's authenticity and soulfulness. From the heart, he shares his spiritual journey to higher consciousness."

RABBI DAVID AARON
author of *The Secret Life of God* and *The God-Powered Life*

"The timing of this book could not be more imminent. Moshe delivers with such candid transparency and vulnerability real-life practical and dynamic approaches in *The Three Conditions*."

LES BROWN
motivational speaker

"This book should reach millions, because millions need it."

RABBI MANIS FRIEDMAN
world-renowned author, counselor, and speaker

Praise for
It's All the Same to Me

"Thank you for your contribution to this field . . . Lots of gratitude for adding this contribution to the world's enlightenment."

DEEPAK CHOPRA, MD

"We live in a tumultuous time, with unprecedented stress. We are all desperate to find words of reassurance and comfort. Moshe Gersht has made us a great contribution with this book."

RABBI ABRAHAM J. TWERSKI, MD
author of *Angels Don't Leave Footprints*

"Spreading this wisdom in the world for others is freaking awesome. Whether people tune in to the universe for health or wealth or joy, it's all the same to me. I appreciate you being out there with the message."

BOB DOYLE
featured in *The Secret*

"Moshe Gersht is sincere. It's a spiritual pleasure to engage with the wisdom of his mind and love of his heart."

RABBI DAVID AARON
author of *Love Is My Religion*

"Impacting, saving, helping, and enriching people's lives. . . . A must-read!"

RYAN HOLLINS
NBA veteran, ESPN sports analyst

"Moshe Gersht presents a clear insight into the quality of mindful equanimity that can make all the difference between living in constant stress and living a serene life, no matter what the circumstances. Of course this is easier said (or written) than done, but this book points the way."

RABBI DR. AKIVA TATZ
author of *Living Inspired*

"Although the concepts are intrinsically deep, it is presented in a manner that is easily understood. An effective means to gain a proper perspective that will enable one to live a happier, more productive, and more Torah-oriented life."

ZEV LEFF
rabbinical communal leader

"The next level! *The Power of Now* meets *The Power of Torah*. Awesome guide to real inner work and exactly what the world needs right now."

RABBI DOV BER COHEN
author of *Mastering Life*

the *three* conditions

Also by Moshe Gersht

It's All the Same to Me

the *three* conditions

how INTENTION, JOY, *and* CERTAINTY *will* SUPERCHARGE YOUR LIFE

MOSHE GERSHT

sounds true
BOULDER, COLORADO

Sounds True
Boulder, CO

Published 2023

Cover design by Charli Barnes
Book design by Meredith Jarrett

Printed in the United States of America

BK06729

Library of Congress Cataloging-in-Publication Data

Names: Gersht, Moshe, author.
Title: The three conditions : how intention, joy, and certainty will
supercharge life / by Moshe Gersht.
Description: Boulder, CO : Sounds True, 2023. | Includes bibliographical
    references.
Identifiers: LCCN 2023003270 | ISBN 9781649631374 (trade paperback) |
    ISBN 9781649631381 (ebook)
Subjects: LCSH: Attitude (Psychology) | Intention. | Joy. | Certainty.
Classification: LCC BF327 .G38 2023 | DDC 158.1--dc23/
    eng/20230622
LC record available at https://lccn.loc.gov/2023003270

FSC
MIX
www.fsc.org
Paper | Supporting
responsible forestry
FSC® C103098

10 9 8 7 6 5 4 3 2 1

Contents

Introduction

It All Started Out like a Dream

Much like many kids growing up in Los Angeles, I dreamed of being a rock star, and when I was thirteen years old, I started writing and performing as the lead singer of a pop-punk rock band. Overall, I spent seven years living the rock-star life, touring and opening for some of my favorite bands. My dream had manifested itself, and it was really all a kid could ask for.

At the release party for our debut album, a good friend asked me a question that changed my life: "Hey, man, how long are you going to do this for?"

"Do what?" I said, still smiling as we celebrated with family and friends.

"You know, play music?"

What kind of question is that to ask a musician? I thought.

I responded, "I don't know, until we're successful, and then I guess I'll settle down and start a family."

"When is that?" he pushed on.

A little more than irritated, I asked him, "When's what?"

"When is successful?"

I'd had enough and told him to grab another drink and bug off. But I woke up the next morning with that question still burning in my mind, and I didn't have an answer. I'd never thought about it before. I was just living my life using the talents I'd been given, having fun, and going on a quest to become a world-famous rock star.

1

It wasn't long after that that I stepped into a deep existential search for my life's purpose and what success actually meant, and I made the hardest decision of my life. After seven years of making beautiful memories with my best friends, record label, managers, and agents, living a life of touring and being on the radio and MTV, I left the band and went on what Viktor Frankl calls "man's search for meaning." Following my heart left those closest to me broken and angry, and although I wish I could have left without causing anyone pain, I knew I couldn't live with the inner knowing that if I stayed, I would be choosing comfort over truth. In the coming pages of this book, I look forward to sharing the answer I found to that burning question: What is success?

You can change your entire life today if that's what you really want. This is the gift of being alive. This is the gift of being human. Over the last decade or so, I have had the privilege of studying Torah, the synthesis of psychology, philosophy, theology, ethics, spirituality, and metaphysics, and I must say we are very lucky. We live in a golden age where we have access to all of the most amazing wisdom. When it comes to expanding our minds and hearts, there are simply no excuses anymore.

There are so many opportunities to find and develop a connection with the inner dimension of life, be it a religion such as Christianity or Islam, a spiritual path such as Buddhism, or something more contemporary such as *A Course in Miracles* or new age spirituality and self-help. You can also walk through the door of science and quantum physics. My entry point was through the lens of Judaism, the metastructure of Torah, Kaballa, and Chasidus. In addition to studying the profound depths of the Torah tradition, I feel blessed to have learned from many of the great masters in the field of spiritual consciousness and self-development. However, which gate you walk through matters less than where you're going. When you dig all the way to the innermost point of every spiritual tradition, you'll find they all lead to the same place: the placeless. My desire in writing this book is to help you access your already beautiful and light-filled life, regardless of your race, color, or creed.

I walked off the stage of my last concert, gave my best friend a hug, and said, "We'll make it through this," to which he said, "No. We won't." Taking the sting of those words with me, I got into a car and headed straight for a flight to Jerusalem. I was going to study in a yeshiva, a school that focuses on the study of Torah wisdom, and I fell deeply in love with the richness of what Torah is all about. The ideas were deep and alive, they were meaningful and relevant, and the most important thing for me was that they validated so much of how I viewed and experienced spirituality. I knew this was a huge part of my calling, and I was compelled to follow where it led.

Over the next twelve years, I devoted my life to digging deeper and deeper into Torah's vision of human spirituality, psychology, self-development, and general metaphysics. I fell in love with Kaballa and Chasidus, which emphasize self-actualization and the elevation of consciousness. I began to develop and give lectures on my favorite topics, working with large groups as well as one-on-one with people who wanted to take their spiritual practice and education further.

I once again felt like I was living my dream.

Breakdown Followed by Breakthrough

Then I had a spiritual ~~breakdown~~ breakthrough, a real dark night of the soul. It started when my first child was born. What do I mean? Well, if you have kids, you likely already know where I am going with this, and if you don't, please don't let this discourage you from having children. I love my children with all of my heart. I have more love for them than I could ever express, but let me tell you, the challenges they opened up for me were on another level. At night my wife and I were up almost every hour or so, there was incessant crying, the bills were getting harder to pay, and my personal time was disappearing more and more by the day. I was stressing about everything and everyone.

But in truth, it really had nothing to do with my kids and everything to do with me. Turns out, I had a big ego.

It's true, the children may have triggered the series of events that followed, but it was *my* interpretations and reactions that perpetuated the problem. You see, I knew it intellectually, but I hadn't yet internalized the spiritual truth that everyone is given the exact set of circumstances they need to proceed to the next stop in their spiritual evolution. These situations just happened to be mine. In fact, when I look back today, I realize that my inner disrepair had very little to do with my children and much more to do with what I allowed myself to believe. I had a whole gamut of limiting beliefs that seemed to be scripting my life.

I was subconsciously weighing exactly what I had to do to be successful and what I had to do to be worthy of praise. Children triggered the part of me that had to deal with what happens when I don't have the luxuries of time, energy, and sleep. I believed I needed those luxuries to accomplish all the things I thought I had to do to be a success.

Things didn't get better before they got worse.

Over the ensuing years, I put on over sixty pounds, developed stress-induced psychosomatic symptoms in different parts of my body, suffered from bouts of rage, and felt constant guilt about my reactions and behavior. I also experienced anxiety and depression, and in the wake of this, I began to truly feel like a failure. I had lost myself.

The peak of this strange series of life circumstances was a turn of events I couldn't possibly have imagined. I dedicated year after year to my spiritual development, and nevertheless, I was hit like a ton of bricks with the realization that I felt more distant and disconnected than I had ever been. I had lost touch with my sense of inner guidance, my intuition that I had relied upon so heavily throughout my youth. I had a difficult time understanding life's hardships, I stopped seeing synchronicities in my day-to-day life, and I felt a total estrangement from what I call God.

Now, this was terribly disturbing because, remember, my day job was to study and teach spiritual ideas that, at this point in my life, I wasn't experiencing anymore. I would walk into a lecture and wow an audience with oohs and aahs of intellectual wizardry, and then I would come home and collapse on my couch in pain from the deep feelings of shame and failure. I took solace in food. I neglected my body, and my energy levels dropped dramatically. I was so lethargic, I found myself sleeping in most days of the week. Oh, and if that weren't enough, my financial situation wasn't thriving either.

Here is the scary part: nobody around me knew. Outside my marriage and my very close circle of friends, I was actually viewed as a great success. To my peers and mentors, I was a scholar, a published author, a great lecturer, a mentor, and a prolific songwriter. I had a beautiful and supportive family, and I was well established in my community. Nevertheless, the pounds kept coming on, the anger wasn't dissipating, I still felt loads of shame, and I was unaware that I had created an imaginary tower to success that I was desperate to climb.

Knowledge Is Only Potential Power

What I didn't know yet was that even though I was plowing through book after book, attending lecture after lecture, and developing relationships with some of the most notable figures in my field, I was still intellectualizing most of the ideas I was learning; I wasn't living them. I had garnered quite a wealth of knowledge, yet I felt as if I'd found very little power.

You see, I was always under the impression that knowledge is power. I found out the hard way that, unfortunately, this isn't always the case. Much of the time, knowledge is *potential* power and the *application* of knowledge is power. If we don't apply what we learn, we end up being smarter people with the same set of issues. Understanding alone isn't enough, but the knowledge is there, waiting for you to use it. Information is just a seed in your mind. What makes it grow is your inspired action.

Accessing your power isn't a small task, but it may be your most important one. It is the first step in the liberation of your soul.

Author and world-renowned medical intuitive Caroline Myss addresses this in her book *Anatomy of a Spirit* when she says, "Power is essential for healing and for maintaining health. Attitudes that generate a feeling of powerlessness not only lead to low self-esteem, but also deplete the physical body of energy and weaken overall health."[1]

Myss explains that inner power is cultivated by a belief in your self-sufficiency as opposed to an external source. When you believe your power is attached to something outside yourself, the moment you feel it slipping away, you begin to lose energy and the power to live your life at the highest level.

> Power is the root of the human experience. Our attitudes and belief patterns, whether positive or negative, are all extensions of how we define, use, or do not use power. Not one of us is free from power issues. We may be trying to cope with feelings of inadequacy or powerlessness, or we may be trying to maintain control over people or situations that we believe empower us, or we may be trying to maintain a sense of security (a synonym for power) in personal relationships. Many people who lose something that represents power to them—money, or a job, or a game—or who lose someone in whom their sense of self or power is vested—a spouse or lover, a parent or child—develop a disease. Our relationship to power is at the core of our health.[2]

It is clear that shifting our beliefs and attitudes about life is the center point for accessing our inner power, and no amount of knowledge without application will ever achieve this.

At this very low point in my life, I was in a frantic search, looking everywhere for a way out of this dark space that I had, in essence, created for myself. I didn't want to numb the pain with food anymore, and I missed my intuitive self-knowledge and inner awareness of the Oneness that exists and pervades all of reality. I knew I had fallen asleep. I had fallen unconscious, spiritually speaking. I was ready to return to my higher Self, the Truth of who I am, but I didn't know how to get there.

If it wasn't for my best friend and partner in life, my wife, I don't know if I would have made it out the way I did. I am blessed to be in an awesome, loving, and committed marriage. She not only afforded me the time and ability to spend nearly a decade of our marriage studying and researching the depth of reality, but she supported my process and growth and held space for me the entire way.

I spoke with my rabbis and mentors, sought therapy, and met with a number of spiritual guides and mediums, searching and digging everywhere I could to find the answers to my life's riddles. In the process, I found a lot of answers, but I also found many new questions and people who resonated with my story in their own way. This book is the answer to those questions.

Let me explain.

Many people feel trapped in their lives by something they don't even know how to describe, and worse, they don't know how they got there. Many of us are in pain and will do just about anything we can to relieve it.

The metaphysical text *A Course in Miracles* says that every communication is either an extension of love or a call for love. This is exactly what Chasidus says about the thoughts we have in our mind. At their core, every thought we have is either an extension of our inner light or a call for help. Every time we try to numb our pain, we're really calling for safety, peace, and love. I was no different.

Awakening from the Shell of Fear

Even though I had all the information at my fingertips, it was only through personal experience that I underwent a transformation. The breakthrough didn't happen until I was willing to take an honest look at the mental agreements I had made with reality and question how I really felt about life. At some point along the way, I had sold my inner knowing of Truth for the trophy of fitting into a mold. I didn't even know there were different molds in the world of spirituality, but I found myself cornered in a space where I was convinced I couldn't fully express the colors of my *Self*.

I realized that if I were to fully jump into the stream of the life that I wanted and deep down believed in, it would likely confuse and offend some people and possibly cut off certain relationships I spent years developing. I knew my social status and integrity might both be questioned. But for the first time, I understood that none of that mattered. I was starting to wake up to a new reality.

As I explored the twelve steps of the anonymous programs that were founded with the intention of helping cultivate authentic spiritual experience, Shula, my therapist, took me on a deep journey into my *Self*, one that I am eternally indebted to her for. In a life-changing session, she looked at me and asked who I would be if I'd taken a different road when I hit one of the forks in my journey. Upon answering her, I saw immediately in her face that she knew something very important.

"You're Chasidic!" she exclaimed.

Although Chasidism is a denomination of Jewish practice, what she meant was "Your heart is in another world. You're not living the life you want to live." I was mesmerized by her clarity, as it immediately resonated. I didn't know what the next step was, but I knew it was needed.

In the aftermath of my awakening, I took a trip back to Los Angeles, where I hadn't been in over a decade. I hoped to make peace with someone who had been my best friend and touring manager, whom I had abandoned all those years earlier. He wanted nothing to do with me. He wouldn't even sit down for a meeting. Later I found out that he wasn't the only one who had those feelings, and some people held a strong grudge against me for what I had done and how I had done it. It was a very painful trip but almost like an act of grace because I came to the harsh realization that there were people in this world who really didn't like me. But that was OK. My understandings of life and my life experiences met, like a wedding between my heart and mind.

This event was significant because of what it meant. As a chronic "people pleaser," I had just experienced what it meant to die. That is, my closest friends truly hadn't forgiven me, people still hated me, yet I was OK. I was still standing. I had made the right decision for myself all those years ago even though people around me were upset by it. Somewhere in my subconscious, I knew that I now had the freedom to do the same, and this time without fear. Even if I decided to shift the direction of my life—my behaviors and expressions—if the shift was in alignment with my higher Self, following my calling, it wouldn't matter if my new family, my new community, would accept me or my decisions. Somewhere deep inside, I now knew that there is nothing to fear when it comes to following your heart and soul.

After over ten years of studying and searching I finally understood the essential idea of all spiritual teachings. Yes, I read, watched, and attended lectures of the great thinkers of our generation, and although my clarity expanded, I started to feel closer to the Truth only after I tasted it myself. This wasn't an intellectual understanding or an emotional reality but rather a deep resonance of Truth that reverberated throughout my entire being. I was free. The wall separating me and everything I knew to be true was gone. The cloud had lifted. The darkness had passed.

What was it? What was holding me back from living my most authentic, powerful life?

Fear.

That was it. I was living with a perpetual subconscious fear. Not the type of fear you have if you're standing in front of a hungry lion but the fear that whatever you're doing will never be enough. The fear that things may not work out for you. The fear that your life is unstable, and anything you do can and will be used against you. The fear that if you mess up, the entirety of the responsibility and blame is on you. The fear that what you wear, how you speak, and what you read and discuss label where you stand in society. The fear that whom you know and what credentials you've received are what define your level of success. Fear is the culprit of all the negativity that we experience in our lives on this planet. Much of our collective consciousness is buried in fear, and our sympathetic nervous system doesn't know the difference between the survival stress of staring down a lion and the human-created stress of getting an MBA.

I can't pinpoint exactly which elements of my personal transformation caused it, but after years of introspection, meditation, spiritual exploration, and therapy sessions that taught me how to forgive and fully accept myself, something miraculous happened. My wall of fear was removed, and for the first time, I truly felt a sense of "I don't care anymore," which really meant "I don't fear anymore." You see, I was living in something that Kaballa calls "the shell of the world." When you live in the shell of the world (the outer experience), you perceive only the external reality as the truth.

No matter how much you intellectually think of things spiritually, if you still identify strongly with the external reality, you won't experience the inner truth of the world, and you will be caught in the shell. When you live in the shell of the world, you live as a shell of yourself. And when you live as a shell of yourself, you live in a man-made hell, a mental space of fear that there isn't enough (a scarcity mentality). A fear of the finite and failure. The fear of pain and death. That is what drives the insanity of the shell of the world. It happens when we believe more in the body than in the soul, more in the world than in spirit, and more in judgment than in acceptance.

That day in LA changed my future. And of course, it wasn't just the one day. It was years of study, practice, and pain. It was learning the core program of the twelve steps and therapy. My teachers believed in my growth. And most of all, I was helped by the love, support, and faith of my wife. But it was on that one day, like an act of grace, that I felt the wall come down, and what I experienced as miracles started flowing in.

The Lightness and Joy Were Radiating

Unexplainable things began to happen left, right, and center. The first thing I noticed was that everyone around me kept commenting on my light energy. It was true—a lightness and joy radiated from me. Things didn't seem so serious or heavy anymore. Although humor had never been my strength, I was now making jokes, and they were actually funny (and not just by my own standards). I will explain what happened next in my chapter on synchronicity, miracles, and manifesting, but as a result of this positive and joyful energy, the circumstances in my life also began to shift.

New job opportunities and speaking engagements started coming my way almost weekly, I sold more books with fewer lectures than in any previous year, and money was coming in from avenues I hadn't thought possible. In addition, my appetite shifted to healthier choices, and the weight started coming off.

The synchronicity in my life was unbelievable. For example, one morning I heard about someone I hadn't seen in eight years, and a few hours later, he walked into my office. Another time, I was considering creating an audiobook, and the next day, at a social event that I had actually not planned to attend, I met someone who told me he made audio- and e-books for a living. In yet another instance, my wife mentioned a neighbor who had lived in our building a couple years prior, and the next day that neighbor called me to say he was in town and wanted to meet for coffee. Whatever I picked up to read seemed to find a number of pathways to enter my consciousness. Life seemed to be happening "on purpose." It was a positive energy storm, and I was in the middle of it.

I was so awestruck by the nature of my energy and the unfolding of my life that I wanted to understand what was happening on a deeper level. I turned again to studying, reading, and rereading any and every kind of book on spirituality, self-development, energy, and healing. My days were filled with turning the pages of the Talmud, Chasidus, and Kaballa, and my evenings consisted of new-age thought leaders such as Eckhart Tolle, Deepak Chopra, and Wayne Dyer. It was a weird yet inspired time for me. I am attracted to and fascinated by the ancient traditions just as much as I enjoy learning from our living teachers. This allowed me to bridge timeworn ideas, concepts, and tools with language that resonated in a modern world. I found a new community of like-minded Torah thinkers who not only validated the experiences I was having but also provided incredible insight and clarity into how and where to channel this newfound energy.

I happily tested and applied all of the wisdom I had garnered without holding back, and the results were awesome. As I will discuss in the chapters on intention and joy, living in perpetual gratitude, meditating, engaging in authentic prayer, and setting intentions became my morning rituals. Studying and conversing about consciousness, love, and light were daily delights. I was enjoying all aspects of my life, from the grand ideas to the seemingly trivial chores of folding laundry and washing dishes. The best part of all of this was my relationship with my wife and children. There was so much more palpable joy and serenity in our time together. In fact, it became easier to find more time to spend together without the feelings of stress that used to accompany being home instead of "accomplishing" something else.

In addition, my intuition was being rejuvenated, and I started sensing and knowing more information about people and events. In many respects, I started feeling like my old self again, but this time with more refinement and maturity. The first couple of insightful moments felt like good guesses, but the more they happened, the more they felt like a familiar wink from a new spiritual reality.

My energy was through the roof, and it was during that period that I gained clarity about how I wanted to spend the next decade of my life. I wanted to share the secrets and wisdom I had found.

My Unique Part in the Majestic Tapestry of Wisdom

I sat down to collect my thoughts and write down my findings on spirituality and living an inspired life. As I began writing, the thoughts in my head hummed to the tune of *Moshe, why are you writing this? Aren't there thousands of self-help and spiritual books out there?* Everyone involved in the world of spirituality has already written about the ego and our human mission to rise above it and transcend into our spirit consciousness, so I wondered what on earth I would be able to add to this cosmic conversation.

I closed my eyes and entered a state of quiet before I sensed the answer arising within me. The truth is that's true. There are many books and speakers, but there is only one of each of us. My understanding of and relationship with the Infinite and spirituality are, in themselves, unique, and thus the lens through which I see the world and my choice of words will be the first of their kind. With this conviction, I humbly decided to enter the arena of the great leaders and thinkers who went before me and add my unique perspective to the majestic tapestry of wisdom, love, and truth.

I hope to open your eyes to ideas you may never have heard or instill deeper within you the ones you already have. I hope to offer some guidance based on my knowledge and experience and help shine light on your road to inner freedom, true success, and fulfillment. I have seen miracles in my own life and in the lives of others I have had the pleasure of working with. What I know is that the spiritual principles that run this world work.

In a religious sense, the ancient paths have always had their own way of describing spirituality, its laws, and the mode of conduct needed to experience the Divine. There are, however, several basic principles and ideas that all religions and spiritual paths agree upon. This book points to these principles. Although I am far from being a scientist, it is amazing and encouraging to see the continual unfolding of science pointing back to these fundamental ideas that run through the life energy of every major religion.

Science and religion used to be in a sort of conflict, with science focusing on the effect and religion focusing on the cause. However, today, most scientists agree that we have entered a new age with the emergence of a worldview that nurtures and illuminates the totality of life through an open-minded study of both the physical and metaphysical. In *The New Physics of Healing*, Dr. Deepak Chopra beautifully expresses that, through the lens of quantum physics, we have overthrown classical Newtonian physics and the superstition of materialism. We can now look at a flower and see it for its external beauty while also understanding that it is made up of energy that moves at the speed of light. Everything is energy. The borders of separation that kept the intellectual from exploring the mystical have melted away, and the miraculous has begun to reveal itself as natural.

Being Ready to Receive

But where would I begin? One day in early fall, I felt ready to receive the insights into what direction I should take in sharing these life-changing spiritual principles. I clearly recall grabbing a pen and paper and writing down that I was ready to receive the clarifying mental download that would be a game changer in my life and the lives of many others. I signed a sacred contract with the Universe.

And then something happened that changed everything. Two days later, on an afternoon before the Jewish New Year, Rosh Hashanah, I was reading a book by Rabbi Yisrael Meir Kagan, who is culturally referred to as "the Chofetz Chaim" or "the Lover of Life," in which he describes a custom performed on the eve of the New Year. With many different fruits and vegetables on the table, each person picks one up and makes a positive wordplay on the food as a prayer. For example, one could pick up a date and say, "It should be the will of the Almighty that we merit to *date* the right people this year."

Although it is a seemingly innocent custom, for the first time, I realized the profundity of what this pointed to, and I was enchanted. He was describing creating the fertile ground for a deep spiritual experience, a training ground for how we see everything that enters our life. Food is the metaphor for that which is shortly going to become the energy we experience. When we view and speak about food as a vehicle for connection, we totally shift the way we experience life.

Rabbi Kagan goes on to say that there are three conditions involved in cultivating the power of this experience: intention, certainty, and joy. When I read these words, my whole world lit up. This was the secret.

1. **Intention** is the choice to live and experience the Truth of who you are. *Choose your authentic self.*

2. **Certainty** is the knowing that the Universe is always directing and assisting you in experiencing the Truth of who you are. *Know that you are always being led.*

3. **Joy** is the feeling of happiness, peace, and love that acts as the barometer of how aligned you are with intention and certainty. Emotions don't lie about what you're thinking and believing. *Feeling good is feeling God.*

You see, for all those years prior to my personal breakthrough, I had been under the impression that all you had to do was change the way you think about things. That changing your thoughts would, in fact, immediately change your life and produce powerful results. Changing your thinking *will* change your life, but slowly and over time. The life you live when your thoughts are charged with the electricity of the three conditions (intention, joy, and certainty) is a quantum leap from just thinking positive thoughts. This is when it becomes life-changing.

Thinking positively can often act like a Band-Aid, covering up negative thoughts and making you feel good for a while. However, unlocking these three conditions can make your good thoughts both sustainable and energetically powerful. Instead of just thinking the thoughts, you will experience the truth of them. It's like the difference between thoughts outside of meditation and thoughts you receive during or after meditation. They feel different. They feel alive. They feel real. In lockstep, you feel amazing. Feeling good is feeling God, and when you're plugged in, your behaviors, relationships, and synchronicities all become elevated.

Before going through my personal experience of spiritual growth, I could never have appreciated the words and ideas on these pages. It was only through experiencing those challenges that I was able to taste the sweet light. These three conditions are the foundation of all the miracles in life. In that moment, I knew this was the starting place for those looking to take the next step in their spiritual journey. These are not just nice feelings you're supposed to have while participating in a New Year custom; they are the fundamental principles for living life.

Intention, joy, and certainty can afford you true inner freedom, a lifetime of success, and the experience of fulfillment. I am filled with great excitement at the opportunity to share them with you. This is the beginning for many and another great step for many more.

The Next Level of Our Collective Journey

Many people I meet describe feeling unhappy, confused, and spiritually disconnected. Often they feel like their spouse or partner doesn't understand them, and they feel alone. Even if they are not in a relationship, they feel the same. Many are unhappy with their job or feel that they don't make enough money. Often they feel that things just aren't turning out the way they wished they would. They feel insecure, tired, and unappreciated. Many struggle with anxiety or depression. Many are angry at God. But what I've learned is that we are all given tailor-made circumstances that force us to wake up, grow, learn, and develop.

I am not a doctor or a miracle worker, and I certainly can't change your life circumstances, but I might be able to help point you toward the *life* behind the life circumstances. My hope is that we can travel together to the next level of our spiritual journey, and if you're reading this right now, that means we've been paired for this shared experience. As with my own experience, my blessing is that you are able to apply the ideas in this book.

One of the main reasons people don't apply what they learn is that the message isn't clear. Complexity is the enemy of application. When things are complicated, we lose the forest for the trees. We can get so caught up in the details that we lose our motivation for action as well as a clear path for movement. Chip and Dan Heath, authors of *Switch*, explain that even if you excitedly share the information, if you can't shape the path, it won't stick, and people won't act. Thus, while maintaining the depth and richness of the wisdom I desire to share with you, my goal is to make this as simple as possible so you can take this information and change your life *today*.

Another reason people don't apply the information they learn is that often their immediate thought when learning new ideas is "I already know this." Many of the concepts I will share with you *should* sound familiar. My intention isn't to reinvent any wheels, just to present the same old ideas in my new way. When Tony Robbins gave his first seminar in Israel, he told us that "people know what I do, but they don't do what I know."

I want you to know what I do *and* do what I know.

There are several things I did for you, the reader, in writing this book. Although I personally resonate with the word *God*, today, for a number of reasons, that word has become something of a taboo because it has been misused and misinterpreted for millennia. There are many ways of expressing the same truth toward which the word *God* points, and I will interchangeably use the words Love, Universe, Presence, Infinite, Truth, Life, and God to describe and refer to the indescribable nature of the immeasurable. It doesn't matter if you call it God, Hashem, Allah, the Infinite Field of Potential, Source, or Spirit. What matters is that we're speaking about the experience of It and not the idea of It. This will be discussed further in the chapter on certainty.

The word we use to describe the Essence of Love is there as a placeholder to help us discuss the same infinite, loving presence that surrounds us and is within all of creation. Perhaps the God you grew up hearing about isn't the God that is. Perhaps the God you do not know yet is something far more expansive and miraculous than you could ever imagine. For the sake of being aligned with the experience of Truth, I prefer that as many readers as possible relate to and connect with the ideas being presented in this book. The words matter far less than the experience. In several places where I quote directly from scripture, I will translate the word "God" as "Love" or something similar.

There's a great story about the Lubavitcher Rebbe, the most recent leader of the Chabad Chasidic movement, who was once approached by an atheist who said, "I don't believe in God."

The Rabbi looked at him and said, "Me neither."

Shocked, the visitor said, "But how is that possible? You're a rabbi?"

He smiled and responded, "The God you don't believe in, I don't believe in either."

The Torah word for God, referred to as *Havaya*, means the eternal present or timeless reality. The closest experience we have to knowing the truth behind the word itself is the truest expression of infinite, unbounded love. At the apex of human experience is the process of alignment and connection with the source of this cosmic, high-vibrational energy that is embedded in the fabric of creation, of that from which everything comes and is perpetuated by, guided by, and returned to. It was all once in a state of no-where. Now, it's all present in a state of now-here. Eventually it all returns to no-where, but it's all from, of, and to the same force that is the force of creation.

Another word that is commonly misunderstood and misused is *miracle*. Normally when people hear this word, they think of something supernatural and magical. It seems like something out of a *Harry Potter* book. In Kaballa, there are two types of miracles: open miracles and hidden miracles. An open miracle is an obvious breaking of physical reality with no natural causes, as in *Harry Potter*. Hidden miracles, on the other hand, can be described as any experience that reveals a deeper unity and spiritual alignment that results in more good, more love, and more light. This could be as powerful as experiencing perfect synchronicity that sets off a chain of events and leads to abundance, your soulmate, or the job of your dreams. It could also be as simple as a mindful moment of shifting from frustration and annoyance to acceptance and forgiveness. Simply put, a miracle is any experience that raises you above the natural order of things. This will be explained further in the chapter on miracles.

I also specifically make a point throughout the book of using the original Hebrew and Kaballa system only when I feel that it is helpful to you, the reader. Although I could fill these pages with some of the most profound wisdom imaginable, so much relies on understanding the fullness of the Kabbalistic system, which is far beyond the scope of this book to even try to convey. Therefore, I have done my best to creatively weave these immensely powerful ideas together in a language that is digestible for all readers who are interested in bettering their life, regardless of their spiritual background and faith.

The Torah system is so vast, it would be a crying shame to think for a moment that this book covers even a small fraction of what the Torah itself contains. There have literally been millions of pages of ink spilled on the subject, and I am adding only a few. I choose to focus on several ideas that I think are crucial and central to all spiritual growth, but by no means does this reflect the vastness of Torah.

The World Will Be Filled with the Knowing of Love

As we prepare to jump into the fullness of this book, I am inspired by the verse in Isaiah that says, "The wolf will dwell with the sheep . . . for the world will be filled with the knowing of God."[3] To know God is to know your deepest and highest Self. To know good. To know peace. To know joy and gratitude. To know Being.

To know Truth. To know God is to know Love. To live a life that is filled with the joy of miracles.

We are not only meant to *feel* happy, peaceful, and loving; this expansion of consciousness is exactly what we're doing here. Your sole business in life is to attain God-realization. You might even say your sole business is your soul business. In learning to know Love and embrace ourselves fully, trust in the unfolding of our lives, and bring joy to all of our experiences, we will energize the way we think and speak and live the miraculous life we're destined to live.

You don't have to believe what I believe. But if you do what I do, you'll get the results I've gotten. I hope this book proves to be worth the investment of your time and that you are moved to live a more deeply empowered and enlightened life.

All the blessings will follow.

part one

the Principles *of the* Three Conditions

Wherever You Think,
You Are

The Full Range of Human Experience

The most important thing at any given moment of your life is your state of consciousness, meaning your energy, the way you feel, and your perception of reality. When you feel good, you think better. When you have good energy, you bring that lightheartedness and joy into your conversations and relationships. When you perceive the world as being on your side, you don't take life so seriously, and you can be more optimistic and playful as circumstances unfold. Your whole life will reflect this truth. See, your natural state feels like love, joy, and peace. It feels free and inspired, and it helps you experience the world as a place of blessings and limitless opportunities. This state, however, may be covered up by fear, false beliefs, negative thinking patterns, and a worldview shaped by the life you were born into. Together, we will journey toward removing the veil and pave a path toward returning to your Self and your source energy so you can experience your best life.

You deserve to have access to the full range of your human experience because life is short. We get a handful of years to live the life we're destined to live, and now is the time for us to create the life we want to live. What I have found through my personal experiences and by studying the world's religions and spiritual paths, psychology, and the ancient wisdom of Torah is that when you change the way you think, you change the way you live. This paradigm is the foundation upon which all inner awareness and spiritual awakening take place because your life takes place in your mind first. Your beliefs shape your thoughts, which shape your reality. My hope is that you walk away from this chapter with a clear understanding that *what you believe is what you'll receive.*

In the following pages, we will dive deeply into the three stages of what I call the Map, an outline of our consciousness and the human condition. As with any map, when you learn how to read it, you'll know where you are, what direction you're headed in, and the exact location of your destination. Also, if you take a wrong turn, you'll be able to quickly get back on track toward where you want to be. And where is that? The unconditional happiness of your natural state.

Whenever you use a map, you start with where you are in the here and now. From there, you can move forward in several ways. For instance, if you notice that your world is in disharmony, meaning you feel emotions such as anxiety, frustration, or sadness, you can most likely follow that feeling back to disharmonious thoughts about yourself or your life situation. When you see the disharmonious thoughts, you can be sure they are backed by disharmonious beliefs. The underpinning of a disharmonious belief is fear—fear of death, loss, failure, abandonment, and more. This belief is out of alignment with the truth of who you are and all that is. Why? Because your essential Self is perfect. Your essential Self is a spark of God, literally a ray of light from the Infinite that is timeless, unlimited, and immensely powerful. Your essential Self, then, is beyond death, loss, failure, and abandonment.

You can also use the Map when you are experiencing harmony in your life. If you follow this feeling back to its source, you'll most likely find harmonious thoughts and beliefs that are in direct alignment with the truth of who you are and all that is—alignment with the source energy of love.

However, you typically have to pick up a map only if you don't know where you're going or if you've gotten lost. The same goes for this Map. You can use the Map when you've forgotten how to get to where you want to be or if you find yourself lost in disharmony. When you start to feel or experience negative emotions or exhibit behavior that doesn't match the person you know you are and want to be, the Map will show you that your thinking and beliefs are out of sync. At this point, you're given a choice. You can choose to stay in disharmony, or you can adjust your thinking to something more positive and loving, something that gives you relief from your current state and aligns you with your true nature. Keep in mind, though, that course-correcting to match the coordinates on a map can take effort. Sometimes you'll need to pull over and reassess your position. There are times when the momentum of your negative thoughts is so powerful that the best move is to focus on anything but that, or simply stop thinking altogether and sit in silent meditation until the momentum slows enough that you naturally feel ready to turn toward love and positivity.

Let's draw the structure of the Map so you can begin to implement it into your life.

1. **Feeling:** A feeling is the way your body energetically reacts to your perception. A feeling of disharmony, then, is a feeling that can range from something as subtle as unease to something as dramatic as anxiety or hopelessness. The first step in using the Map is recognizing that you are simply not feeling good. This is a warning sign that you're not living in complete harmony with the essence of who you truly are. This feeling of being misaligned with your true Self is the source of all emotional unrest and confusion. But how did you get out of alignment in the first place? Your mind tends to seek out boundaries, explanations, and limitations that allow you to then label everything. These mental constructs are not your true Self. Rather, they're all the thoughts, opinions, and stories

you've projected onto life, and in making them, you've *forgotten* your true being and become caught up in the outer layers of your existence. This is where disharmony begins. As I will explain throughout this book, the goal is to awaken and *remember* the truth of who you are, which will help you return to harmony and alignment.

2. **Thought:** Thoughts are the ideas, concepts, memories, words, stories, images, and opinions that take place in your mind. Every experience has an ancestor in thought. If you feel it, then you've thought it. At any given moment, you are thinking thoughts that either support or challenge alignment. Moments or periods of disharmony—the feelings of step one—are the results of thoughts that are dissonant with who you truly are. Moments of alignment are generated by either thoughts of alignment or the complete absence of misaligned thoughts. Simply creating space between thoughts also brings us back into alignment.

3. **Belief:** Belief is just another form of thought. However, it is a thought you have had so often or in such an impactful way that you now immediately take it to be true rather than consciously thinking about it. This isn't your subconscious but rather unrealized conscious thought. You may not even realize what you believe about life. You may have never consciously thought about or addressed the beliefs that drive the way you live. In this way, your beliefs are one step closer to your essence. They sit on the nexus between your consciousness and your experienced reality. They are like the first layer of clothing, closest to your skin but covered by other layers. You could be wearing a loose-fitting sweater and jeans, but if that first layer underneath is uncomfortable, you will be walking around feeling uncomfortable all day long. If elevating your thoughts will change your moments, elevating your beliefs will change your life.

Beyond belief is only a deep, true, indescribable knowing. Words can only point back to the knowing, never fully capturing it. It is your essential Self, the real you beyond the forms and limitations of this world, the you behind the curtain of your life—your spirit, your presence, your soul, or simply consciousness. The *you* you think you are, you are not. And the *you* you think you are not, you are. I describe this concept of Self and the ways to access it more fully in my book *It's All the Same to Me*.

Stage 1: The Loss of Inner Harmony

What is the loss of inner harmony? The very first story in the Torah acts as a perfect metaphor for this idea. The Talmud elucidates the story in Genesis about Adam and Eve in the following manner: man and woman were created as a single entity, back to back. Then, God split one from the other and charged them with the mission to reunite with one another. The beginning is unity, and the end is unity. It is only in the time between that things are experienced separately.

Most people have a misconception that this story is strictly speaking about a man and a woman. In reality, this story plays out within every one of us. You see, we have the qualities of being creators and achievers as well as experiencers of love, peace, freedom, and joy. We all have two different energetic powers within us. One of them is associated with *doing*, while the other has more to do with *being*. One has to do with *creating* and the other with *consciousness*. It is the difference between *action* and the energy of *flow and allowing*, the difference between the expression of *achievement* and the experience of *wholeness*.

One of the most astounding elements of the metaphor is the names of our characters. In Hebrew, Adam is related to the word *adameh*, which means "I will become like." Eve, whose name in scripture is Chava, is related to the word *chavaya*, which means "experience." Thus, the names "Adam" and "Eve" quite literally mean the two aspects of becoming and being, expressing and experiencing. Put simply, Adam and Eve represent the two parts of our human experience: the desire to express our innate creativity and power in the world and the essential experience of consciousness feeling its way through life.

So we're left with this message: we were all born with the power to achieve greatness and be creators in our lives, yet we all have the innate desire to live with joy, love, and peace and experience wholeness and fulfillment regardless of what we accomplish. However, we have been split in two—the separation of the soul and body, the mind and heart, a *mental* divide between the way we judge and analyze life and how we live and experience it.

The imbalance between these two opposites is the source of disharmony. By putting so much focus and attention on how well we can climb the ladder of success, we lose the joy of being alive in the process. Yes, of course I want us all to be externally successful in everything we do, but my measuring stick for success has dramatically shifted in recent years. At the end of the day, success without fulfillment is failure.

When we were children, both parts of our inner world were still somewhat married to each other. We were able to feel happy and fulfilled despite our performance and achievement or lack thereof. In fact, we experienced a much greater sense of joy because we didn't have anything we, in fact, actually had to *do*. We could simply *be*. Just enjoy. Just have fun in the moment, with the moment.

That stage, however, doesn't last very long. Very quickly our pure nature is inundated with parental and societal nurture. Our perceptions become molded by the thoughts, judgments, and opinions of others, and we enter the rat race known as life. We interpret all of these things and make assumptions about life. Our assumptions give rise to judgments and biases, and we learn to distrust others and compete for the title of "best." Attention becomes our greatest reward, and our ego-driven desires become dominant. In just a few short years, the emphasis shifts from presence, satisfaction, and enjoyment to achievement and attention-seeking at any cost. In an effort to rise to the top, judgment and fear become our driving motivators. In this, the calling of our soul becomes ever more of a faint whisper, and we begin to fear and forget who we truly are.

Essentially, this progression is the basic nature of your entire existence. Before life, you are one with the Source and the infinite potential of life. Then you are seemingly split off, individuated, and created as a separate entity. In your perceived separateness, you forget the true nature of your being: an eternal, never-ending light of love and potential. When you don't feel this truth, you feel small, weak, alone, and vulnerable. A subliminal, existential fear becomes the underpinning, driving force of your life, and you adapt by trusting the "big people" you're surrounded by as a child. It seemingly might have been better not to go through this splitting process, but in contrast to the initial unity, you now have the opportunity to reunite with the Source energy from a place of conscious choice and independence.

The story of Adam and Eve represents a cosmic divorce we have undergone between these two dimensions of our once whole inner self. The main objective of this book, and hopefully of our life, is to find our other half, our true soulmate—innate joy, love, and a trusting spirit—and marry the two halves of our being into one. We can create a united outer world only if we learn to live with unity from within.

Stage 2: Your Thoughts Create Your Moments

Although, the human mind is universally accepted as our greatest tool in shaping our experience of life, it can just as easily be our archnemesis. It can be a loving friend as easily as it can be a wicked enemy. On the one hand, we credit the human mind with developing, creating, and manifesting our greatest achievements. On this exact point, Napoleon Hill said, "More gold has been mined from the thoughts of men than has been taken from the earth." On the other hand, much of the world's chaos is a result of the nightmare this tool has created.

We've all gone through times when our lives were wrecked by our negative thinking about ourselves or others. As we will explore in the condition of certainty, the negative, fear-based thinking of the mind is created when we mistakenly believe that we are in complete control of our life's circumstances and events. This is when the mind starts taking over your life. You start to feel as if you are responsible for the bad results. And when life doesn't go your way, you become frustrated by the outcomes. The mind stops being a tool that you use and instead becomes a tool that uses you. Every challenging situation has this internal and mental struggle of interpretation attached to it. Our minds' reactions to life's conditions are often the very things perpetuating the pain we deal with.

It's time to start changing the way we think.

When You Change the Way You Think, You Change the Way You Live

We act the way we act because we feel the way we feel. We feel the way we feel because we think the way we think. Thus, when we change the way we think, we change the way we feel and act, and in the end, we change the way we live.

As such, life is an opportunity for transformation.

Do you know what it means to transform? *Trans* literally means to go beyond, to elevate and rise above. *Form* means limitation or physical state. When you elevate the way you perceive the world, i.e., the way you look at yourself and others, you transform your life and go above and beyond your self-imposed limiting beliefs about yourself and the world around you.

We are all on a journey of transformation to fully experience and express who we really are, and a huge portion of this journey is taking place in our heads. That's where we are "living," so to speak. The founder of the Chasidic movement, the Baal Shem Tov, said, "Wherever you think, you are."[1] Think about that sentence for a moment. *Wherever you think, you are.* Well, where do you want to be? If you want to be in blissful love and joy, you have to think blissful, loving, and joyful thoughts. That could be as simple as saying, "I am good enough, and I deserve love," or recalling great memories with your best friends. If you want to be in anger, irritation, and sadness, you have to think those kinds of thoughts. Again, it can be as simple as saying, "I hate this; things never work out for me," or lingering on the memories of all the bad things that have happened to you throughout your life.

The physical space and circumstances you're in have very little to do with your state; they're almost like an afterthought. It's mentally labeling the situation that makes it feel the way it feels. We will always be challenged by life. The choice is ours as to whether we embrace this reality. You can't choose the specific events of your life, but you can choose what you focus on and how you interpret them. You can choose *how* you see what's happening. There is a whole world that exists behind your eyes. Always remember that what's happening in front of your eyes is not as important as what's happening behind them.

Living Your Miracle Mindset

Do you know what the rewards are for transforming your thinking? Freedom! Freedom to feel happy, joyful, peaceful, loving, and enthusiastic. Freedom from the inner agreements about your life that keep you from experiencing the real you. Now you can go out into the world with a smile on your face, caring less about the opinions of others than about what your soul truly calls out for, what you really want. King Solomon, known for his deep and poetic insights and wisdom, said, "As you think, so shall you be."[2] Changing your thinking changes the way you *feel*. It changes your inner state. It changes your *entire existence*. It can take you from feeling miserable to feeling a powerfully positive, high-energy, loving, radiant, joyful, grateful, and peaceful state of love and harmony.

You are equipped with the miraculous power to radically change your life in an instant. Knowing that you direct your thoughts and that your thoughts shape your reality will open up a world of possibilities. I call the highest level of this awareness a "miracle mindset." A miracle mindset is thinking in ways that are supportive, loving, hopeful, trusting, and open to infinite potential and possibility. Some of the feelings associated with this mindset are joy, a sense of peace and security, enthusiasm and inspiration, and general positivity and contentment.

The miracle mindset accesses the power of your being, your true presence and true nature, allowing you to feel the experience of alignment. It opens you up to the idea that there is a pattern of thinking that aligns you with a deeper truth about yourself and reality as a whole. When you live with a miracle mindset, you don't just perceive things a certain way; more importantly, you *feel* a certain way—namely, happy, lighthearted, and peaceful. These feelings are the expression of an inner alignment with the higher Truth— that which, from a pure state of consciousness, you'll know and naturally experience. This higher Truth is something people often channel in meditation. The miracle mindset, then, acts as a bridge connecting you to that feeling state, which impacts every area of your life. The feeling isn't the goal so much as it's the barometer for how strongly you believe in the thoughts you're thinking and the ideas you're trying to identify with.

The Garden of Eden is known as the place where Adam and Eve ate from the tree of good and evil. But there was another tree in the garden, the Tree of Life, which symbolizes our authentic connection to God, Truth, and Source Energy. It is our higher consciousness. If we call living with a miracle mindset and living in alignment being connected to the Tree of Life, then the following are where its BRANCHes extend in your life: **B**ehavior, **R**elationships, **A**ttraction & abundance, **N**egation, **C**hanneling & creativity, and **H**ealing.

1. **Behavior:** When you feel good, you behave differently. You are more productive; you act with clarity and precision; you are nicer, friendlier, and more positive in situations and outcomes; your actions and reactions

to life's situations flow seamlessly; and you make better choices. You're also more flexible and confident. Why are all these the results of the miracle mindset? Because we make choices based on how we feel. We can always justify and rationalize our decisions, and as a general rule, we do what we want. The heart is king. Feeling good is the most important decision you can make. Feel good first. The miracle mindset is a bridge back to the natural feelings of love, joy, and peace.

2. Relationships: People can instantly feel your energy, and when it's uplifted, it can immediately strengthen communication and connection. It isn't just because your behavior is nicer; it is actually the energetic effect of being near someone who's in a truly positive space. When you are deeply connected to Consciousness, to God, you are present. You elevate the entire room without saying a word. People may not even realize that it's happening or why, but they are drawn to you. They desire a relationship with you and are more likely to be influenced by you. When you align with your natural sense of inner joy, your influence expands and your energy becomes magnetic. This alignment shifts the energy of your home, sharpens your ability to make new relationships and business deals, and brings peace to those who are struggling. Your presence instills calm, leaves others feeling energized, allows people to feel better about themselves and part of something bigger, inspires a sense of purpose, and builds people's trust in authentic personal connections.

3. Attraction and abundance: The Zohar, an ancient Kabbalistic text, explicitly states that the world shifts for us and leans in our favor when we are happy and positive. Our mental state and emotional reality define our vibrational frequency and thus what we draw into

our lives. That includes the people, experiences, and things that correspond with how we feel. Abundance follows abundant thoughts and feelings. Love follows love. Joy follows joy. That is why we experience tremendous synchronicity when we're in the right mental space. The powerful Wayne Dyer statement "If you change the way you look at things, the things you look at change" isn't just nice wordplay. It is reality. In *Think and Grow Rich*, Napoleon Hill writes, "Our brains become magnetized with the dominating thoughts which we hold in our minds, and, by means with which no man is familiar, these 'magnets' attract to us the forces, people, and the circumstances of life which harmonize with the nature of our dominating thoughts."[3] This is why a miracle mindset attracts all forms of abundance and a miraculous life.

4. Negation: When you're in a powerful state of positivity and light, you don't just bring good energy to a room; you actually negate and soften negative energy. Lower energy vibrations and frequencies can't stand in the face of higher ones. The Baal Shem Tov poetically explains that this is the meaning of the verse "Mountains will melt like wax before God."[4] The mountains of negative thoughts and energies can't stand in the light of Godliness and higher consciousness. You become an island of peace in what others would consider a chaotic sea. It is almost as if you are walking within an invisible bubble that repels negative forces. Misery likes company, and that means it won't like being around you! When we have the miracle mindset of light and love, nothing negative and destructive in the world can get in our way.

5. Channeling and creativity: When you feel good in your high-energy state, you become a channel for divine insight. You can receive new information and creative ideas more easily and become a clear conduit for miracles and

spiritual guidance. The world will literally bend for you and your intentions as you receive obvious divine messages. In this state, your intuition is heightened and your ability to contribute to the world is multiplied.

6. **Healing:** Aside from happiness having been clinically proven to enhance the healing process, all spiritual paths universally recognize that being happy and in a peak energetic state has potent healing properties. Through the power of a miracle mindset and the joyous energy it engenders, people all around the world, throughout all of history, have experienced cures and healing from life-threatening diseases, anxiety, depression, and even ailments as simple as headaches, pulled muscles, and the common cold. The way you feel changes the way your body heals. Healing doesn't refer just to the recovery of the physical body; those ailments are often physical manifestations of something happening within. True healing occurs when one's spirit releases a long-held fear and/or negative thinking pattern toward oneself, others, or life. This healing is activated by living in spiritual alignment through the miracle mindset.

You have the ability to live the life you want to live; build the relationships of your dreams; attract incredible abundance; negate all negative energy; channel insight, wisdom, and guidance; and heal yourself and the world around you. This is the promise of shifting your level of consciousness. This is the power of reconnecting to the joy of your life. This is the outcome of marrying your inner soulmate and unifying the truth of your *Self*.

What is the only thing that is really in your control?

Your conscious thinking.

Your whole life depends on how you think. You are the creator of your life. Imagination is the clothing of the spirit. So what do you want to wear today? I would try on the miracle mindset and see how it fits.

The way you think is habitual, and the good news is you can change your habits. You become what you practice most, and therefore, as you think, so shall you be. The chapters that follow will take you on a journey of learning to form new habits of thought so you can successfully integrate the miracle mindset into your everyday life.

Chasidic Master Rebbe Nachman of Breslov writes,

The most important thing in your life is how you think—to guard your mind from negative thoughts and to fill the space with Goodness. Your mind is the space through which you create the world you live in. When you fill it with negative thoughts, you have destroyed your world. What a foolish way to live. When you think a negative thought, you block your mind off from your connection to the Infinite (the Universal Energy of Love and Good) and lose your joy. However, when your thinking is good and positive, you live in alignment, which brings healing and draws miracles into your life. In this state of alignment you receive new insights, wisdom, and information that you couldn't have otherwise perceived. You draw energy, abundance, wealth, and blessing into your life.[5]

Practicing these beautiful and powerful words will produce the fruits of their promise. If you sow the seeds of the wealthy, you can expect to produce wealth. If you sow the seeds of the joyful, you can expect to produce joy. If you sow the seeds of the spiritual, you can expect to produce spirit.

You were created with the potential to sculpt your world. A proverbial verse in the book of Psalms says that in the end of time, we will collectively awaken from our spiritual slumber and will say, "We were like dreamers."[6] This is the secret to waking up. You get to dream the dream of your life, so dream a beautiful dream instead of a nightmare. Success comes to those who are success-conscious.

In the same line of thinking, goodness comes to those who are good-conscious, miracles come to those who are miracle-conscious, and Godliness comes to those who are God-conscious.

Stage 3: What You Believe Is What You'll Receive

We would all love for it to be this easy. Think a happy thought, feel a happy feeling, and now be the greater version of you. Unfortunately, we know it's not that simple. Positive thinking is extremely important, but there are some prerequisites to energizing the power of your mind.

First and foremost, it's important to know that we are dealing with two minds: the conscious and subconscious. Your conscious mind produces what you think about at any given moment. All the thoughts streaming through your brain, including daydreams and analytical thoughts, are part of your conscious mind. Your subconscious mind contains your beliefs and inner agreements, your worldview, and your paradigm for perceiving reality. From moment to moment, your conscious thought is generated from your beliefs, the stimuli in your environment, or your habitual use of your mind.

The subconscious mind is what sets the stage for how we *experience* reality. It dictates how we feel, which is why some have called it the "feeling mind." It is within this mind that we have agreed to a certain set of limiting beliefs about ourselves, others, and the world at large, and it is *this* mind that keeps us trapped in the pain of the past and worry about the future. This is ultimately what holds us back from experiencing the truth of who we are and living the miracle mindset.

We are made in the image of our Creator, which means we ourselves are artists. The most important work we create is our ART, our Automatic Response Thinking. Through agreeing with and believing in certain "truths," we create a painting of how we see reality, which is the way our brain automatically responds to life's circumstances. These paintings were created by us as children. As adults, we can now paint a new picture by reprogramming our beliefs. One of the ways to do so is to shift our conscious thinking. Simply changing the thoughts in our heads would be a good start, but what really runs our system of thinking is our paradigm of how the world operates and how we see ourselves and our function in the world. So we think the way we think because we believe what we believe. Knowing this is the beginning of awakening and transforming our lives.

This brings us back to the three conditions: alignment with yourself (intention), trust in a loving Universe and the present moment (certainty), and the steady flow of joy in your moment-to-moment experiences (joy).

Believing you can create your own life starts with addressing and challenging the most basic beliefs you have about yourself and life. Over the following chapters, we will dive into what could become the most exciting time of your life. You'll become aware of what's really behind your way of thinking, what's keeping you from doing the things that resonate with your essence, and what's fueling your limiting beliefs. Together, we'll understand that you won't be happy when you have a good life. You'll have a good life when you're happy.

You have the power to totally shift the way you experience life, and when you do, the life you experience will totally shift. The problem is we often find ourselves stuck in a mental story we've been telling ourselves for years. These stories have become the mantras we carry with us throughout our days. They may sound like, *This always happens to me. I always mess things up. If I don't get this done myself, it won't ever get done. Nobody really cares about what happens to me.* These are stories about ourselves, others, and the world that ultimately dictate how we feel about life.

Although it's somewhat foolish, we have been raised to believe that it's totally normal and expected to turn life and its circumstances into a problem. The truth is that every problem we think we have has a spiritual solution because, in the grand scheme of things, there are no problems, only life situations. We create "problems" with our minds. It is the way we think about the situation and what we believe about life that turns situations into problems. Is it a problem when you spill coffee on your shirt on the way to a meeting? No. It's simply a circumstance. It's how we think about the coffee stain, judge ourselves for being careless, consider the judgment we might receive from others, and all the other thoughts *about* the coffee that turn it into a problem.

Einstein said that you can't generate a solution from the same mind that created the problem. He was so incredibly right. You can't find the solution to a problem when you still see it as a problem. Only when you change your attitude—your inner experience of what's going on—will you become a clear channel for new insights and ideas to enter your mind.

The only real problem you can have in this life, if you can even say that, is becoming separate from your Source. Separate from your Self. Separate from God.

The following story points to the nature of the inner change I am talking about. A woman was attending a spiritual retreat and was asked to write her life story in five chapters on five separate note cards. What she wrote was the following:

- **Chapter 1:** I was walking on the street, and I didn't notice a hole in the ground, and I fell in. I said to myself, "I don't know how this happened. It's not my fault," and I sat there a long time, not knowing how to get out.

- **Chapter 2:** I was walking on the street, and I *noticed* the hole in the ground, and I fell in. I said to myself, "I don't know how this happened. It's not my fault," and I sat there a long time, not knowing how to get out.

- **Chapter 3:** I was walking on the street, and I noticed the hole in the ground, and I fell in. But this time, I said to myself, "I know how this happened. It's my fault," and I was able to get up quickly.

- **Chapter 4:** I was walking on the street, and I noticed the hole in the ground, and I was able to avoid it altogether.

- **Chapter 5:** I walked down a different street.

Let's choose to walk down a different street and come to a new way of thinking, a new level of consciousness, a new way to live. I invite you to be bold and courageous. It may require you to step out of your comfort zone and be open to the words and wisdom written on these pages. Remember that as you read on and apply the ideas in this book, you will experience an inner shift of positive energy and the BRANCHes of having a miracle mindset.

Choose your presence. Choose alignment. Choose the real you.

After we develop the three conditions of intention, certainty, and joy, we will revisit the power of thought, speech, and action from a new perspective. These are our tools and modes of expression for engaging with the world and actualizing our human potential. What's holding us back the most in our lives is being unplugged from the unlimited potential of our soul. Through realigning with the Truth of who we are, what we are a part of, and what we can do, we will supercharge all of our actions to create the true meaning of success: the inner marriage between the two parts of our soul.

The three conditions are what allow the mind's power to accelerate and create the life you want. They address your reality, your emotional state, and the inner agreements you have with yourself. By shifting the two most important beliefs you have, coming into alignment with the truth behind those beliefs, and experiencing your natural state of joyous peace, you can become a superchannel for love and miracles in your life. You can become a magnet for success and gain access to energy, healing, and power you didn't even realize you had. Divine guidance and abundance will fill your life, and all of the things that seemed insurmountable and in the way will seem to move to the side, opening the road to the version of you that you want to experience.

CHAPTER TWO

The Condition of Intention

Go to yourself. Go for yourself.
—GENESIS

Harmonize with the Truth of Who You Are

The single most important element of experiencing your dream life is clearly knowing your intentions for living. This will directly enhance your spiritual empowerment. In the introduction, I discussed the inspiration for this book and quoted Rabbi Yisrael Meir Kagan, who said there are three conditions to accessing your inner power. The first condition is intention, what he calls *Teshuva*, meaning the intention to "return to your Essence" or look inward and return to your *Self*.

Living with intention is a decision to live in harmony with the truth of who you are rather than according to someone else's judgment. It is your ongoing and active choice to remain aligned with your innate goodness, love, creativity, health, spirit, divinity, and deep connection to life's blessings. In this mode of living, you'll find yourself turning everything and everyone in your life into allies who will help you carry out the grand intention or purpose of your life.

Do you recognize that within yourself, there is already perfection? When you face the direction of your true authentic self, it starts to become obvious. You return to the Source of who you are, your inner perfection. All of life is a movement toward the realization of this perfection. It is all about returning. It is all about remembering and awakening to this truth. Before you were created, you knew with absolute clarity what life was all about. It was only after birth that you started to forget the true nature of your connection to the Infinite. There's a part of you that won't ever forget and won't let you fully forget, and that's the part of you that you're returning to.

A Perfect Extension of Love Connected to All, Separate from Nothing and No One

People travel all over the world to search for themselves. But you don't need to go to India, Rome, Mecca, or Jerusalem to find yourself because there is no place you are not. In fact, just like the Soul of the world, you are *placeless*. Have you ever thought of that before? Being placeless?

What do I mean?

The Truth is we are not physical beings who periodically have spiritual experiences. We are actually spiritual beings journeying through a physical experience. Our essence is part of a universal whole, a Oneness, the interconnectedness of all things. Some call it our soul, spirit, or God. Others call it the energy of the Universe or simply the Universe. It doesn't matter what you call it. What matters is whether you experience the Truth of it. To know this reality is to feel part of something that is both immeasurable and indestructible. You are forever. You are safe. You are OK. You will come to understand and sense that you are one with something eternal and infinitely strong, something beautiful and creative, something free and inspired, something that is perfect as is and perfect in becoming more. Know that underneath the physical appearance of things, you are one with all that is.

As you experience joy, peace, love, confidence, and total acceptance, you will have a deep knowing that you have a divine purpose in this world and you are part of the greatness that is life—a feeling that is truly freeing. You will feel beautiful and perfect, as you are part of the beautiful perfection of the world. This is what it means to truly feel at one with your essence.

I love Rabbi David Aaron's expression: "Everybody wants to feel like a *someone* because deep down we all know that we are *some of that One*." Plainly and simply, you are an extension of love that's connected to all and separate from nothing.

The Truth is:

1. You are **Good**: Your essence is pure, and in the deepest sense, there is no evil in you. Ecclesiastes says, "God created humankind straight,"[1] meaning humans are innately in alignment with the essential good that is the infinite love of God. You are good because you are part of God.

2. You are **Safe**: Your essence is alive and never dies. You are eternal and indestructible. You are not your body, your achievements, or what others think of you. You are forever. You are timeless.

3. You are **Perfect**: Your essence is one with something infinite and purposeful. All of your apparent imperfections are divine gifts assisting you in your purpose in this lifetime, and they are perfect, as are you. When you realign with the Truth of who you are, your soul knows no imperfections, only the joy of being part of the Great Perfection. You entered this physical dimension to add more perfection that it didn't or couldn't have before you showed up—and by the way, you are doing a great job.

4. You are **Creative Love**: Your essence has boundless love to give to the world. You are born with a unique genius that only you can express. The creative way you bring light and love to the world is what makes you you.

5. You are **Connected**: Your essence is connected to all that is, including everyone you meet, everything you can see and touch, and everywhere you go. A profound togetherness unifies us, and you have the ability to elevate those perceived as "others" when you elevate yourself. There are no others, just people and things that look that way.

Before you were born, you knew this. In fact, this was *all* you knew. Life as we know it has persuaded us to put our faith in the body and believe in our purely physical experience. But, just for a moment, I want you to imagine that you really know this. Who would you be if you knew in your heart that you were good, safe, perfect, and here with a unique mission of expressing love and goodness with your creativity? What would you do? How would you live? How would you treat the people in your life? When you are in harmony with this truth, you feel so good that you can't help but be a loving, joyful light to everyone you meet, everywhere you go. You love what you do and do what you love. You are awake.

Imagine if you always knew you were good, not based on what you did or how you looked but just because you *are*. Imagine not having to live in constant worry about your life and instead knowing deep within that you are truly OK and death isn't the end of your journey. This does not have to be a distant reality for you. You can know this. You can have this. You can live this.

A Shoe Called You

Ninety-nine percent of who you truly are is invisible and untouchable. To put this in perspective, imagine that the name you have, the personality you've developed, your career, your health, and everything you do is all like one of the shoes you put on every morning before you leave the house. We'll call it *the shoe called you*. Now, imagine that a person about your height has their foot in this shoe. They have a head, a neck, a torso, arms, and legs, and at the very bottom, they have two feet, one of which is sitting snugly inside this shoe called you.

Your true Self is like the body, which is so much bigger and infinitely more intelligent than a shoe could ever be, and yet its foot fits perfectly in this shoe called you. The vast majority of who you are is so much bigger than anything we can imagine. Now, just for a moment, consider that until now, you have basically convinced yourself that you are only the shoe and nothing more. You're convinced that when your laces become untied, your life is over. Until you can go beyond the boundaries of form and realize that this is not who you are, you can never live the life you're capable of living and create the miracles you're capable of creating.

I am here to remind you that you are perfect just the way you are. You have boundless gifts and potential. You can help others and make the world a more beautiful place if that is what resonates within you. The world has been waiting for you and what you are meant to bring to the table. The day you were born was the day God decided the world couldn't exist without you anymore. And that is still true every day you're here.

False Evidence Appearing Real

Growing up, I was taught that we are all born with a tabula rasa, a clean slate. Well, it may not be exactly as clean as they say it is because, in truth, we all have natural traits and strengths that have little to do with our nurture, our surroundings, or the innate challenges that we come into this world with. Nobody's package is the same, but we are all the same in that we each have one. Nobody has the same spiritual purpose, but we are all the same in that we each have one of those too.

As children, we enjoy the gifts of being alive for a quick minute before we are then impacted by our surroundings. We develop a belief system based on what we're told, and we're *told* that certain people are good and others are bad. We're *told* that we are successful only if we are good-looking, rich, popular, and have many achievements to speak of. We're *told* that we are a grade on a piece of paper and that it's more important to have a good career than a good marriage.

These are the things we're *told* by the way our societies behave. We are taught to judge, and judges we become. Even if we have never heard anybody literally say these words, subconsciously, this is the message that we receive. If we're not busy, then we're lazy. If we're not stressed out, then we're not working hard enough. If we're not dating, we're ugly and unworthy of love. If we're not rich, we're failures. We live within these mental guidelines, these self-limiting beliefs about life, until they betray us, and through this "blessing in disguise," we're forced to either change what we believe or fight to justify those beliefs to the death and die with them intact.

In addition to what we pick up from others outside us, we are impacted by what goes on inside us. By nature of being in a physical body with physical senses, we naturally lean into the physical experience with the notion that that is all there is. We believe the physical is all of who we are and that it is the only space of existence. When our five senses have thoroughly convinced us that everything that exists is physical, we agree with them and accept this version of reality. This furthers our tendency to forget our true essence.

It's no surprise that by the time you're reading this book, you likely experience yourself as a body that can think about spirituality if it chooses. The reality, though, is exactly the opposite. You are a spirit that can express itself through a physical life you have chosen. Life starts us off separated from this inner knowing so that we can find our way back. It's like the story I mentioned earlier of Adam and Eve. We are separated so that we can use our free will to reconnect.

The inability to feel our deep, divine connectedness and perfection as a self-evident reality creates the space for the illusion of separateness. You think you're the shoe! You perceive yourself as an isolated part, a fragment that is weak, limited, and alone in the world. This gives rise to all the fear you feel in your life. Instead of experiencing yourself as good, safe, perfect, loving, and connected, you see yourself as potentially bad, in danger, imperfect, unimportant, unworthy of love, and separate from everything and everyone. This is a catastrophic mistake. FEAR occurs when you take this **F**alse **E**vidence **A**ppearing **R**eal as the truth and forget that there is so much more to who you are.

Of course you will experience an underlying feeling of fear if you see yourself only as a physical being. That means you can be injured, and it also means you will die. If you acknowledge only the physical, your life won't have any objective meaning, and if you are small, you will believe you are indeed weak and susceptible to danger. Life will simply be survival of the fittest.

It is this underlying fear that leads to living a life where you have to climb the ladder of success and do whatever you must to get ahead. That may mean being immoral, lying, or sacrificing your integrity. Fear becomes a driving force in your life. You experience scarcity instead of abundance, thinking there isn't ever enough and that if you don't prove yourself to the world, you yourself are not enough. You have to do everything in your power to be the shining star, to attract attention, to earn accolades and the stamp of approval from family, friends, and society.

In the animal kingdom, if you're weak you're literally dead meat. To you and me, that easily translates into being emotionally and spiritually dead meat. Our world suffers from anxiety, depression, and deep-seated shame. It's easy to become a perfectionist who feels the need to perform and please others in the name of achievement. When we aren't "successful" in the eyes of whomever we believe is the barometer for success, we then try to numb the pain with our media devices, food, drugs, and alcohol, and some numb themselves by going into overdrive at work. It's likely that we have lost connection to our inner Truth in more than one area of life.

For me, this became apparent one Friday night when I was sitting down with my wife for dinner. As our conversation unfolded, I looked at my full bookshelf on my left and saw hundreds of books with countless ideas; inside, I felt this gnawing feeling of impossibility.

"Impossible," I told her. "It's impossible."

She looked at me and said, "Moshe, what's impossible?"

Tears rolled down my cheeks, and I said, "I just don't get it. I have learned and studied and practiced, and yet I feel so far away. Far from myself, far from what I know is true. The books are unending, the wisdom is infinite, and there is just no way I can master all of this."

With deep compassion, she looked at me and calmly said, "Who said that you have to?"

A feeling of serenity washed over me as the clarity set in. There is a part of us that knows the truth. Sometimes you just need someone to remind you. I am so grateful she did, and it snapped me back to reality. There is no prescription or number of books that you have to read and master. There is no information outside you that can tell you who you are. Education is powerful and important, but the ideas contained within the pages are there to serve you and your expansion and help you find yourself and open up to things that might have been forgotten. Feel what resonates. Listen to the stirring of what happens inside when you read the pages. Those are the inner signs of what's truly important.

What is holding us back from living a dream life, a life where we can do what we want and be the person we know we are deep down? At the core of all our layers is unsettling fear. There is certainly something to be said about the toxic habits we've likely picked up along the way, and it requires some real work to unlearn them, but the bars of our cells are made out of fear. We've taken the false evidence appearing real to be true.

Fear, though, is rooted in belief. A belief in the finite rather than the infinite, the limited rather than the unlimited, and the dying rather than the eternal. We continue to believe in judgment rather than acceptance, in separateness rather than unity, and in struggle rather than peace. It is through the lens of fear that we judge others, complain, create drama, and then run to numb the pain with aggression, addiction, and pleasure. Your ego gives you the impression that this belief is serving you, protecting you, and saving you, but in the end it is really keeping you captive. It is the wall between you and your true Self, between you and your spirit, between you and Truth.

When we believe in the fear, we have fear-based thoughts. These thoughts then express themselves as fear feelings and fear responses—in other words, a disharmonious life.

It doesn't have to be this way.

Belief is a choice. We can choose another way. This is the meaning of the verse in Deuteronomy that says, "I have placed before you life and death; choose life!"[2] This is the most important free-will decision you can make: to be more awake, more conscious, and more alive. So here is the great news: you are not stuck. There is a way back to yourself. There is a way back to the uniquely powerful, creative, and joyous Self that you truly are. Setting an intention to follow this journey will be one of the most important things you will ever do for yourself, and it will be your new basis of success and achievement.

The Greatest Sin Is Living Against Yourself

One of the most commonly misunderstood words in religious doctrines is *sin*. You may automatically think of sin as something bad or immoral, but what it really means is to miss the mark or to be lacking. To sin is to miss the point of your life, to lack the whole picture of what it means to be you. The greatest sin is living against and rejecting yourself. This outlines much of the pain experienced in our lives.

There are a number of ways our fear gets the best of us and makes us think, speak, and behave in ways that work directly against our true nature, keeping us from actualizing our great potential and feeling happy, worry-free, and in love with life. When we simplify things, there are only two modalities we can live in: one based in fear or one based in love. We are acting either because of some impeding threat external to us, be it physical, emotional, or spiritual, or from a place of acceptance, enjoyment, and enthusiasm. We're either reacting to an event or making a proactive choice.

Take a moment to reflect on your life. Think about some of the biggest decisions you've had to make—the schools you went to, the career path you chose, the social network you're a part of. What were the motivating factors or reasons? If any of your answers are not to the effect of "Because I love this, and I know I am fully expressing myself when I am there," you likely made the decision because of an external factor. Anytime you don't love what you're doing, you're doing it because of a fear of what will happen if you don't. Intentional choice is synonymous with consciousness, wanting, and love. You are only ever choosing or fearing.

When we live from a place of fear, we're not fully living and not really choosing. We're just fearfully reacting to life. Thus, we're not living in alignment with our power. We're more focused on what could go wrong than on what we actually want to go right. It doesn't end there either. Every negative emotion we experience, such as anger, rage, frustration, depression, or anxiety, originates from that same fear. Our need for control, our insecurities, and our feelings of doubt are all a result of not living in harmony with the truth of who we are.

But remember what I said in chapter 1. Your whole life is really happening in your mind. Every negative thought you've ever had is a response to what you believe. It is either what you believe about yourself or what you believe about your life circumstances that directly shifts the way you live.

Rethink Your Nightmare into a Dream

Remember the Map, our feelings, thoughts, and beliefs? You'll find what beliefs led you to your disharmonious thoughts and, ultimately, all the disharmony you experience from day to day. Another way we can relate to this idea is to call these beliefs the "stories" we tell ourselves. We are all walking around with one of two major stories: a love story or a fear story, a dream or a nightmare.

Your dream may sound something like this: *I believe I am loved, accepted, and desired. People like me. I like me. I am successful, attractive, and able. I have infinite potential. I am intelligent. I am strong. I am wealthy. I expect to fall and learn from my mistakes. I do what I love. I have the power to say yes or no whenever I want to. I have access to great power. I am confident and have integrity. I am always improving. I am never stuck and can always change my circumstances. I am totally in the zone. I have energy. I feel wide awake. My life will unfold perfectly.*

Your nightmare, on the other hand, may sound more like this: *I believe I am not loved, accepted, or desired. I am afraid that people don't like me. I don't like me. I am not successful, attractive, or able. I am afraid I won't be successful. I have limited potential. I am stupid. I am weak. I am poor. I am afraid I will fail. I don't do what I love. I don't have the power to say yes or no whenever I want to. I am afraid of what will happen to me if I assert myself. I don't have access to great power. I can't do anything, and I lack confidence and lie to myself and others. I can't figure out how to improve. I feel totally stuck and can never change my circumstances. I am not in the zone. I am tired. I have no energy. I am afraid that my life will have a sad ending.*

We all have our own unique and specific beliefs about ourselves and life, and it's extremely worthwhile to write them down and get to know them well. When you gain clarity on what's going on under the surface, you give yourself the power to change the story. You can always change your story, but you first have to realize that a story is being told.

When we subconsciously identify with our nightmare—all the fears buried deeply within—we feel, speak, and behave in ways that don't reflect the life we really want, and we step out of alignment with the intention of our life. Thus, we tend to overcompensate or stagnate and do nothing at all. It's all laid out in the Map. When we believe our fear story, we think negative thoughts, feel negative feelings, and act in negative ways.

For example, I recognized that for much of my life, I carried a deep fear that if I didn't perform well, people wouldn't love or appreciate me. On the one hand, this fear motivated me to exceed the expectations people had of me, whether it was in my band, my relationships, or my quest for knowledge. However, what came with it were subconscious thoughts such as *I'd better get this done or I'll be a failure.*

Earlier in my teaching career, students often came up to me and asked questions I didn't know how to answer. In the moment, I felt nervous, and I subconsciously thought, *Oh, my God, if I don't know the answer to this question, I am worthless. I have nothing to contribute.* This, in turn, led me to overcompensate by either defending why I didn't know the answer or quickly putting together a sophisticated-sounding response that maybe answered the question and maybe did not. Subsequently I felt some guilt and washed it down with a slice of pizza (or three), a bag of chips, and a soda. Then I beat myself up for overeating, became angry, and for no good reason snapped at the people closest to me. That is how the nightmare perpetuates itself when we totally believe the fear story, the nightmare of our subconscious.

Do you see how quickly we can go from positive to negative? Somewhere inside, I carried a fear *belief* that I had to be perfect. If something went wrong it was my fault, which made me a bad person and triggered *thoughts* of guilt and shame, which then created *disharmony* in my emotional state and, ultimately, my life.

In contrast, when I sit down with a student today, I am aware that my ability to give a good answer to a question has nothing to do with who I am. I know that I am part of the infinite good, a being used as a channel for love. It is in this clarity and inner knowing that all relationships and encounters become powerful opportunities for love, joy, and connection.

This is the power of living in your dream, living with love, and reinstating the positive and good beliefs about yourself and your life. This is one of the by-products of stepping back into the miracle mindset. This is the secret. When we are in fear, we judge, usually because we are assessing the situation in hopes of reaching a safe space. So we put people down and put others on a pedestal because it creates context in our mind about where we stand and how well we are doing. We think this will give us the feeling of safety. This is also why we often find it difficult to give up the fear we've grown dependent on. We are consumed with staying comfortable. Even if it's wrong, we still feel safe within this fear. That is why we stay in bad relationships, overeat, stay up all night watching Netflix and surfing the internet, and generally waste a lot of time.

There is a part of us that doesn't want to give up the fear. Why? Would you believe me if I said it was because of more fear? We become so invested in our fear story, our negative beliefs about ourselves and the world, that our agreements with reality actually become like an addiction. In this sense, we are resistant to being ourselves. Resistant to being happy. Resistant to choosing peace. Resistant to love. As I said before, our essence is really creative love, and our intention is to return to that place of knowing good, feeling good, and being good.

So what happens if you choose happiness instead?

Well, most people are afraid of what is on the other side of this major decision, but I ask you to notice the resistance. See that there is a part of you that is afraid to let go of your fears, and if you so desire, choose to do it anyway.

You Paint Your Experience of Life

Imagine that the world is the most delicious and beautiful fruit you could possibly envision and is encased in a very pretty, albeit strong, shell. Imagine if you never cracked it open but instead continued to bite and bite at the strong, inedible shell. This is what it's like when we stop living according to our inner truth and what's really important in life and focus more on the material than on the spiritual, more on "who you know" than on authentic relationships. This is the shell of the world, a fear-based reality in which we think our dreams will come true if we just do what the world says. When you live in the shell of the world, you live as a shell of yourself. To live in the shell is to live in a man-made hell. When you make the decision to drop the shell and go within, peace will be yours.

We all look up to someone, and somewhere inside, we may have *decided* that we have to be like them to be successful and worthy of love or acceptance. This is an agreement, an invisible contract that we make between ourselves and the Universe. We're convinced that this must be true because these people represent success, emotional well-being, and spiritual prowess. Nevertheless, it couldn't be further from the truth.

Our mentors and those we look up to are not destinations; they are guiding lights pointing us in the direction of ourselves. You won't ever become your mentors; you will only ever become your-self. They lead the way by being *themselves*. The most important lesson we learn from the great teachers of the world is that what-ever they were teaching, they were doing it as themselves.

The root of the Hebrew word for *believe* (*emunah*) is *amen*, which means "I agree." Your beliefs are your inner agreements with reality. You can, however, reprogram the way you experience your life. You can crack the shell and begin to taste the wonderful fruit of life. When you are stuck in the shell, in the nightmare, it's because you have forgotten your power to create your life. You are the dreamer of your life, so dream a good dream. When you can see the truth of this and drop all of your limiting beliefs, you will be one major step closer to freedom.

Lean into Love

The following words are from the righteous Chasidic sage known as the Maggid of Mezritch, whose writings have deeply touched me: "There are two worlds: the world we see with our eyes, and the world we don't see with our eyes. The latter is a world of love. Choose to live in love."[3]

Your responsibility to yourself is to lean into the love of your life as often as possible. Return to your essence and take time to truly understand your journey of spiritual maturity and development. We always want to move in harmony with the Universe, with ourselves. You'll feel most at peace when you live in total alignment with your soul. Even though we've all made mistakes, deep within, there is an unchangeable healthy core that is untouched by any of the bacteria of self-rejection, distortions, and impersonations we've created.

In trying to figure out why I couldn't seem to lose the extra weight I had put on, I went to several specialists and nutritionists to work out what I could do to help my body. It seemed that no matter what changes I made to my diet, my body was holding on to the weight. This went on for a number of years, and I was tired of getting the same results (and so was my wallet).

One day, I had an appointment with Nili, a nutritionist with whom I was finding some level of success. We sat down, and after a few minutes of questions and going over my food plan, she said, "Moshe, I can see that you have no desire to do anything with this. I know it sounds strange, but until today, I felt you were totally into it. But today, your whole energy is resisting what we're doing." I was surprised because she was absolutely right. I had no desire to be there. I had basically given up again and was ready to stop the program.

She then said, "Look, I am not an empath, but I'm pretty intuitive, and I have a feeling that your problem doesn't have to do with food. This is something more internal. This is something much more fundamental." When I asked her what she thought it could be, she suggested it might have to do with a lack of love. I was surprised. I felt very loved and adored by many people. Nili asked if she could send a picture of me to a friend of hers who had a special gift of seeing the energy of people and helping them move through blocks, even if only through a photo.

Curious, I said, "Why not? Let's go for it."

The next day, she called me and said that her friend had seen my picture and felt that my "issue" indeed stemmed from a lack of love, but not lacking from anyone around me—lacking from myself. I wasn't loving myself enough. Now, when she said that, I really didn't understand what she meant because of course I loved myself. Why wouldn't I? When I tried to probe further about what I could do to resolve this problem I didn't think I had, she said, "Nobody can figure this one out for you. You have to figure this one out for yourself."

I didn't know it yet, but she had given me a tremendous gift. I may have *thought* I loved myself, but in reality, I wasn't *living* that way. I was still totally caught up in the "achieve, become, and impress" model of living. A glass ceiling held me back from my own growth. I couldn't see that there was anything holding me back because on paper, everything looked fine. It wasn't until about a year later that I had a breakthrough realization that I was basically living in fear of what people would think, say, and do if I were to fully embrace everything I am. Once I was able to accept that reality, a cloud lifted in my life and things began to change.

This is what I learned.

Acceptance, Enjoyment, and Enthusiasm

What happens when you let go of fear and lean into the life you want to live? You'll take action out of pure love, not because of the reward you will receive afterward. Even though in the latter case, it may seem as if your actions are charged by desire, they're still actually driven by fear because your reason for them is based on something outside yourself. It's not a bad thing to want results, but you have to remember that the results are not yours anyway. You can only choose what you do in the process.

Do the things you love for the sake of doing them, without any desire for the reward afterward. Make the doing itself the reward. This is the meaning of the line in *Ethics of the Fathers*, "Don't serve for the sake of receiving reward."[4] Enjoy the actions of your life.

Yes, the results will come, the reward will be there, but that shouldn't be why you're doing it. Do it because you love it, and you won't ever need to think of the reward again.

Whenever you feel as if you *have* to do something instead of wanting to do it, that is fear. For example, most people go to work simply to make money, not because they love what they do. Then they take vacation days to escape all the unhappiness they carry from their job. Twelve-step programs all over the world assist people who are caught up in the "work really hard, then escape really hard" cycle. The same is true in your relationships. If you feel that you *have* to be there, it is fear that is keeping you stuck, and this will ultimately create resistance, which will eventually create resentment. This resentment will then turn into hatred for what you do, whom you're with, and ultimately who you are. I encourage you to find a way to take action because you *want* to instead.

In *A New Earth*, Eckhart Tolle describes three modalities that a person living with presence, what I call intention, experiences. At the base level is acceptance. One step beyond that is enjoyment, and even higher up or deeper in is enthusiasm and being called to life by meaning. In Chasidus and Kaballa, these are referred to as "harmony" between the three basic levels of consciousness: *Nefesh*, base personality; *Ruach*, energy or spirit; and *Neshama*, soul or higher consciousness.

Making peace at the level of Nefesh is about accepting reality as it presents itself on the surface without standing in mental contrast to what is. The very first step I had to learn was to drop all resistance to whatever I was doing. If I actually *have* to do something and there is no way around it, I practice accepting it fully. Whether I want to or not, if something must be done, I take responsibility and get it done. I can't imagine anybody *wanting* to get up and change a crying newborn's diaper at 2:30 am, but to resent it is insanity. Another word for acceptance is *surrender*. It isn't a sad picture of surrendering to harm but rather an empowered decision to stop fighting reality. When I surrender to life, I actually feel better and more empowered. When you surrender to your circumstances, doors will open. Act as if you chose your circumstance because somewhere, on a deep level, you did. Try not to make the present moment an enemy. Always make it your friend. Don't stand in resistance to your life. That will only create pain for yourself.

On the level of Ruach, your energy is in total alignment with life and you enjoy what you're doing. You find ways to make life fun, such as going to places you enjoy and surrounding yourself with people you like being around. Taking it a step further, this is where acceptance meets appreciation, and you find joy in both the little things and big things alike, such as quietly walking upstairs to your room while everyone is asleep, washing the dishes, taking out the garbage, or just breathing. When we stop resisting life and start living with intention, we bring our presence everywhere we go and to everything we do, and when that happens, our reality becomes a space of joy.

Sensing the meaning in what you're doing makes life enjoyable and allows you to experience deep and real enthusiasm for it. This is the awakened state of Neshama. The word *enthusiasm* is borrowed from the Greek word *enthousiasmos*, meaning "God within." You are in total alignment with the God within when you energetically do the things you believe you are in this world to do. Nobody has to tell you to do them, and you would likely be doing them even if you weren't being paid. In fact, the primary reason you're probably not doing it is that you're afraid of not being paid for it, but we'll explore that more in the next chapter.

One of my wife's mottos is "Stop living your life as an explanation, and start living it as an exclamation." If you actually like what you're doing, you'll also do your best. The quality and quantity of feeling you have while living your life will shift for the better. You won't even feel as if you're working anymore. You'll have fun. You'll live your life. Living life this way may not feel natural at first. It is like forming any new habit. It takes work, and you'll mess up along the way, but don't stop. You're one positive thought away from creating the life you want to live.

So set this as the new intention for your life. Say it out loud. Write it down. Write a sacred contract between yourself and the Infinite that affirms that you will be true to the light of your highest self, the Self that is loving, good, creative, and unique. Practice thinking those loving, appreciative thoughts, feel the good feelings, and watch how your life transforms in every way. Your life is all about a return to your true Self. When you plug back in to the truth of who you are, you literally become unstoppable.

Intention is about turning inward so you can listen to the murmurings of your heart, the whispers that come from the essence of who you are by nature. If you listen closely, you will hear the wise voice that arises from your inner being and tells you to return to your true Self.

In the next chapter, we'll explore the methods and tools we can use to make the condition of intention powerful and practical. Using the Map, we'll look at how we can reorganize our energy, get back into harmony with ourselves, shift our perspectives, and reach beyond our fear-based beliefs.

CHAPTER THREE

Intention Applied—Bringing Intention to Life

Awareness, Action, and Conscious Contact

In today's world, we seem to care greatly about what other people think and have found countless ways to keep ourselves out of alignment with our inner voice because of it. But deep down, we are part of an infinite field of Love that encourages, enhances, and supports all of life. In this space, we are all creative and kind, and we all want to flourish, grow, and expand. We naturally see the beauty in everything and everyone and live in deep appreciation for life.

I want to show you how this idea plays itself out by going back to the Map of our feelings, thoughts, and beliefs.

> **Beliefs:** Say, for instance, you have a thought such as *I am afraid that if I don't perform at a superhigh level, those I care most about won't think I am valuable.* This equates to *I **believe** that if I don't perform at a super high level, those I care about most won't think I am valuable.* Now, what's the issue with this belief? It's valid, right? Sure, and at first glance, you may not see anything wrong with it. But the problem is that there is a fear-based belief behind this, namely, that this person believes they are valuable only in terms of how other people value them. This underlying belief is the motivator behind the fear of not performing well.

With this mindset, you allow yourself to believe that you are not valuable if you don't perform well. We associate being of value with being worthy, good, and lovable and having purpose and importance. So when we dig deep here, we find that behind the fear of underperformance and not being valued is the real fear that you won't be good, worthy, lovable, important, or purposeful if you don't perform well. Wow. That would certainly motivate me if my entire existence was on the line every time I had to perform. This represents the classic ego beliefs of *I am what others think of me* and *I am my achievements.*

Thoughts: This belief may produce the following common thoughts: *I have to get up early and stay up late to get work done, even if it's going to exhaust me and get me sick. I can't fail; otherwise, I am worthless. I don't have time to spend with my husband or children while I am working on this, even though our relationship needs it. What are my relationships worth anyway if I am nothing? I wonder if there is anything I can do or say that will give me an edge, even if it's not true. It doesn't matter if my heart is not in it; I have one shot at this, and I am not going to let myself strike out, no matter the cost. This has to be my best project yet; otherwise, I am a total failure.*

So what's the result of all this mental noise? These fearful thoughts can drive you to live in ways that deplete your energy, stunt or ruin your relationships and health, and encourage perfectionism and people-pleasing.

Feelings: When you believe these kinds of fears and think these self-destructive thoughts, you'll likely feel anxious and stressed out, which can very quickly turn to anger, rage, and panic if left unchecked. You see, there is no real stress in the world, only people who think stressful thoughts because they live with a stressful belief—in this case the belief that if you don't perform, you don't matter. That belief can single-handedly destroy your life and the lives of your loved ones if it leads you to act rashly by cutting yourself off from people, lashing out at others for insignificant reasons, or numbing yourself with drugs, alcohol, gambling, overeating, television, video games, or anything else that helps you escape the disharmony of living the lie you've created with a simple belief.

If we paid a little more attention in many circumstances of our lives, we'd likely notice that we're living in perpetual fears that may not actually be true, even though we've convinced ourselves that they are. These, in turn, shift our thoughts, feelings, personal interactions, and, ultimately, behaviors. In other words, they shape our lives. The question is how can we use the Map to get ourselves back to the Truth?

This comes with the power of living with intention. It's about shifting the dynamics of your belief system so you can be and experience the most authentic, powerful version of yourself. As we discover more ways to cultivate awareness, bring intention to our actions, and make conscious contact with our inner being, we can step away from the darkness of disharmony and into the light of Love.

Cultivating Awareness

When we attempt to develop awareness, we must consider two distinct aspects. One is *beforehand*, where we can take time to address self-inquiry, and the other is *in the moment*, being present with what is happening now. An idea that really impacted my life is "It is always my best mind that got me here." What this means is if I had had a better way to deal with the situation at the time, I would have! It was only because I was unaware of another way of looking at things or responding that I allowed myself to walk down a street I would later regret. You are hardwired to make the best decision you can with the state of consciousness you currently have. I think it's safe to say you're never trying to get life wrong on purpose (nor can you).

This principle is important for two reasons. First, it allows you to forgive yourself after you've made an apparent mistake. It was your best mind that got you there. And second, it sheds light on the source of poor behaviors. You didn't have a better way of thinking. That was the only way you knew how to cope in those moments. If you had had a better way, you would have taken advantage of it. The bright side is no matter which way you took, it was exactly the road that led you to the self-discovery you needed to make. Acknowledging that you were simply unconscious to another way of reacting and being is really the beginning of awakening. When we behave in ways we later regret, it's important to remember that it was our best mind that brought us to those actions. If we knew better, we would do better.

In his amazing book on cognitive behavioral therapy, *Feeling Good*, Dr. David D. Burns lists ten ways fear speaks through us. He calls these patterns "cognitive distortions":[1]

1. **All or Nothing or Black and White:** "It's *all* bad. I messed *everything* up. They are getting *everything* wrong." Do you hear how fear exaggerates issues and creates unnecessary drama in your life?

2. **Overgeneralizing:** "This *always* happens to me. I *never* get it right. I am going to feel this way *forever*." Using words like *always*, *never*, or *forever* distorts reality and makes your life more dramatic than necessary.

3. **Mental Filter:** "Yes, forty people came to my party, but Jenna didn't; I knew this birthday wouldn't work out. I know it's a brand-new car, but there is a scratch just under the right passenger door; I knew this was too good to be true." Even if everything is fine, you focus exclusively on one negative detail. It's like dropping one drop of black ink into a glass of water. It colors the entire glass.

4. **Disqualifying the Positive:** Rationalizing why good experiences "don't count" with statements such as "It was just a fluke; I never really win. That doesn't count; she was sick. I had extra energy today; it must have been the weather. They're lying just to make me happy." Whereas some distortions turn up the volume on negativity, this one mutes anything positive, leaving you focused on the neutral or the negative.

5. **Catastrophizing:** "It's totally *ruined*. I am going to get *fired*. They *hate* me. I am a *terrible* person. This is the *worst* thing that could have happened. This is a *disaster*." This amplification of life's situations might leave you feeling so overwhelmed that you will be too debilitated to take positive action.

6. **Labeling or Mislabeling:** "I *am* bad, useless, evil, a failure, dumb, a jerk," or any other word you use to label another or yourself. As opposed to looking at the event or actions that transpired, you label and judge the whole of yourself or another person. The situation then becomes nonlocal and thus a generalization of an entire being.

7. **Jumping to Conclusions:** This distortion has two aspects to it. The first is Fortune-Telling or Assuming: "Because X happened, Y is for sure going to happen. They are going to leave me. I am going to lose my job. They are going to laugh at me. I am going to be embarrassed." This mode of assumption leads you to jump to conclusions about life that hinder your ability to see clearly in the present moment. Ultimately, it might cut you off from potential future realities. The second aspect is mind reading: "After what happened, now they are thinking this about me. They are laughing at me. They are mad at me. They hate me. They are trying to get me. They don't think well of me." This is another form of assuming.

8. **Emotional Reasoning:** "I feel it; therefore, it must be true. I feel worthless; therefore, I know I am worthless. I feel dumb; therefore, I know I am dumb." One of the most common experiences is to believe that because you feel bad, you are bad. This emotional reasoning immediately cuts you off from the truth of your being, leaving you identified with the emotion instead.

9. **Personalizing:** Arbitrarily concluding that a negative occurrence was your fault despite having no evidence to support that: "It's my fault she's hurt. I should have called her last week" (even though there was no way you could have known).

10. **Should Statements:** "This shouldn't be happening. They shouldn't have done that. This car shouldn't be parked here. I should have gone there yesterday." When these statements are directed toward yourself, you'll likely feel bitter and self-righteous, and when they're directed toward others, you'll likely feel sour and resentful.

The common thread throughout all of these is that they are fear-based thinking patterns that motivate something I call "compensation thoughts." A compensation thought is what happens after you experience a subconscious fear belief. They are emotions or actions that try to compensate for, and ultimately *fix*, the problem you are afraid of and think you have. They are the thoughts that sound like the following:

1. Judgment, blame, and defense ("It's not my fault" or "I'll get them back.")

2. An attempt to perfect, please, and perform ("I'll prove to you that I am still good enough and worthy.")

3. A need to retreat, hide, and numb ("I am a failure" or "I'm not safe.")

We justify, assume, label, and judge others to feel safe. We're scared to not know, to just ask, and to wait and see what will happen. No matter which thoughts your mind gravitates toward most, there are simply no justified resentments. In the end, you are only hurting yourself.

With this in mind, I want you to study yourself and determine what mental phantoms and beliefs you've bought into, the underlying fears about yourself and life that bring up disharmony. Do you have cognitive distortions that linger in your day-to-day life? Notice what symptoms come as a result of experiencing that fear. Learning to recognize the signs of fear and being sensitive to the language it uses are among the keys to not falling back into its trap. Most of the time, it's just a simple lack of consciousness.

Getting Our Story Straight

Stories: Take some time right now to write your unique story. Answer the following questions on a sheet of paper:

- What are the stories and images that come to mind when you think about the chaos of your life?

- What thoughts do you think when you are feeling lousy and in a low mood?

- Where in your life do you find yourself struggling, and why do you think you struggle there?

- What thoughts do you tell yourself about your struggles?

- Whom do you become when you are in a negative headspace? Take note of which cognitive distortions or compensation thoughts show up most for you. They may point you in the direction of the predominant fear belief that is holding you back.

Now, on a separate sheet of paper, answer the following questions about your dreams:

- What stories and images come up for you when you contemplate all the blessings in your life?

- What thoughts do you think when you're feeling positive, motivated, and joyful?

- How would the best version of you think and live?

Now, look at these two pieces of paper and marvel at the different beings living in your body. It's amazing that we all have a Dr. Jekyll and Mr. Hyde. I know that when I am living with intention, I am happy, positive, loving, encouraging, and enthusiastic about life. I think thoughts of appreciation and love, and I marvel at the beauty of the world. I appreciate the little things and enjoy my breathing immensely. I am inspired by the depth of wisdom I see, and I become a signal that picks up insights and novel ideas that I couldn't have thought of otherwise.

When I am not living with intention, I don't want to be around myself, let alone anybody else. I tell myself all sorts of stories about not being good enough, needing to fit in and be "normal," and fearing abandonment. My thinking becomes distorted, and I almost immediately turn to food or distractions to get my mind off the negative feelings.

When You're Ready to Feel, You're Ready to Heal

Symptoms: A symptom is a sign that something exists, and in this case of living intentionally, it's the existence of harmonious or disharmonious thoughts and beliefs. It's time to start getting to know your symptoms. Every time you believe in your fears more than in the light, you experience negative symptoms in your thoughts, speech, and behavior. The first step in your liberation is to monitor and notice what thoughts you are thinking, what language you are using, and how you feel throughout the day. I started keeping a trigger journal, which is a diary of different scenarios and events that would trigger me as well as the physical and emotional symptoms that would follow. This is a wonderful gift you can give yourself.

The easiest way to witness how much you're living in the light is to gauge how you're feeling. For example, I know I am in harmony when I feel happy, loving, and positive. I find it easy to joke around, and I am lighthearted. I am motivated and inspired and find myself sending silent blessings to people everywhere I go. I am confident enough to make hard decisions with an empowered yes or a strong no. I am calm and peaceful, without worry, and I lean into caring for my physical and spiritual health. I feel totally in flow with the world, receive insight and strong intuitive messages, and witness awesome synchronicities in my day-to-day life. When I am living with intention, I can see and feel people around me being uplifted and moved by our conversations, and life feels meaningful. When I am in harmony with my higher consciousness, I act as a channel for peace and joy.

When I am out of sync, the opposite is true. I feel lousy and am filled with self-doubt. I experience shortness of breath, and I am negative and judgmental. I take myself and everything else too seriously, and I am unable to make decisions. I waste my time watching and reading things that are irrelevant to my intention, make poor decisions about what I should put into my body, and feel justified all the while. I become tired and lethargic and lose my passion for accomplishing anything. I feel disconnected and annoyed, and my energy is dreadful. I find myself alone and without direction and just want to go to sleep and wake up with a new mind.

In my experience, it's important to be just as interested in what is going on inside me as with what is going on in the world around me. We all have a dozen or so repetitive thoughts that we always think when seemingly bad things happen or when we mess up. Pay attention to those thoughts and even more specifically to the language you use when you are in that space. Then do the same when you're in a good mood, feeling plugged in, high, and living your dream, aware that you are living it right and totally aligned with the Universe. What kind of language do you use when you're totally present? What thoughts do you have when you're feeling grateful? Being clear on these things can help you instantly change the story you're playing in your head at any moment.

Make sure you're in touch with your body and emotions. Feeling physically drained, achy, and tired is a sure sign that you are energetically depleted. Fear depletes your energy and is responsible for making you feel emotionally tense, irritated, stressed out, down, or any other negative feeling. These feelings are always an indication that you are likely stepping into the red zone in terms of what you're thinking and believing.

Cultivating this awareness will help clear your symptoms. Start noticing how you feel when you are totally aligned with who you are and how you feel when you're not. What kind of faces do you make and how do you breathe? Do you feel like connecting to others or running away? Does your body get hot? Do you start having urges to eat things you know aren't good for you? Do you feel energized, confident, and calm or tired, weak, and anxious? Do people want to be around you? Do *you* want to be around you? When you ask yourself these questions, be honest. The more you are in tune with your energy, the more quickly you can bounce back when you fall into a lower space.

The Language of the Wise

Another symptom is your word choice. What words are you using? When we start to pay attention to the language we use, we can easily detect whether we're in harmony or disharmony with our thinking. An easy way to gauge whether you're thinking in spiritual harmony is to notice whether you are complaining. Every complaint is preceded by a fear thought that asserts that "*this* shouldn't be happening." You can use complaints as a warning light reminding you that you are thinking fearful, negative thoughts.

When you give energy to what's going wrong, you'll only feel bad and draw more of that type of energy into your life. You don't want that! Nobody does. We mistakenly think that when something goes wrong, it will get better if we complain about it. This is simply not true. Instead of running away from problems or deflecting with a complaint, run toward solutions. Don't march *against* something bad; march *for* something good. When you live with intention, you are naturally solution-focused. Think about what you *do* want and speak about it. Love what you do, and do what you love.

It sounds easy enough, but it's hard to stop complaining once it's a habit. Why, though? Why do we harp on negative situations when we know we should be positive and focus on the good? The answer is that there is a part of us that still believes that complaining, venting, and talking about how bad things are will get us what we want. But what do we really want? To feel good. We're under the impression that we'll feel good if we complain and talk about how hard our day was or what someone said to us earlier that morning. But the truth is it makes us feel bad. Venting is overrated.

If you're ready for change, commit to not focusing on the problems anymore. There is only ever one true problem, and that is a lack of intention caused by a disconnection from your essence, which is good, powerful, and perfect. From now on, focus on your intention instead. Who are you right now, and who are you trying to be? Focusing on what is wrong gives away your power and helps you step into fear. Focusing on what you want instead will allow you to lean into love, reclaim your power, and enjoy your life.

It is true that you may not be able to control every circumstance, but you have considerably more control over your thoughts. You will not be able to fill all situations with enthusiasm, but when you accept them for what they are, you can make the next best decision from a place of peace.

Another form of language that we want to be on the lookout for is name dropping or bragging, those "I knew that already" or "I told you so" moments. It's likely in those moments that you may feel a need for validation and attention, which again is connected to a fear thought. You may want to be the first one to share news, whether good or bad, and for a fraction of a moment, you may feel special because you know something someone else doesn't. That feeds the subconscious fear of not being good enough, valuable, or special.

As part of your new spiritual practice, I suggest trying out the following. The next time someone has something to say and you strongly disagree, don't say anything. Just listen and let them say it. If it really isn't all that important, try to say the most powerful four words you can say to someone: "I think you're right." When you have an opinion about something, but in the grand scheme of things, it doesn't make much of a difference, practice sitting in silence. You may find that diminishing the normal reactions you have to fearful thoughts opens up a space within you that can just be happy with the way things are right now.

One of the best indications that you are back in a fear story is when you are gossiping. In every spiritual path, gossip is considered a toxin that ruins the fabric of society and ultimately hurts no one but the gossipers themselves. If you want to live a good life, guard your tongue against speaking negatively about others. If you pay attention, you may notice that you don't even like it and it doesn't feel good, but it may be hard to stop. It's like when you start eating a bag of chips and at a certain point you don't want them anymore, but you don't stop. You always feel better when you stop. Your body thanks you. Watch what happens to your life when you abandon this habit. Your soul will thank you.

By placing your awareness on these symptoms, you will likely feel an immediate release of some sort. That's because you have somewhat distanced yourself from the symptom and have become its observer instead. This brings you one step closer to your *Self* and to living with intention, *Teshuva*, a returning to Self.

Return to Life

Once you have cultivated a sense of awareness *beforehand* and have practiced being present with how you feel, think, and speak *in the moment*, you can take positive action and start shifting the way you experience your life. There is a difference between the energy of your life and your life circumstances. When you start to see this, you can return to the life you desire, a life of pure and unconditional joy.

Once you've picked up on the "red alert" signals, it's time to do an about-face and return to your presence. Three easy ways to do this are reciting a mantra, using prayer, and taking a breath. By performing these simple acts, you will draw your power back and center yourself.

Reciting a mantra can be incredibly helpful. It can be as simple as "I am," "Spirit," or "Awaken," which all serve as reminders for you to come back to your Self. Alternatively, it can be more detailed, such as "I let go and let You guide me. I invite a new perspective. I choose to shift." The goal is not to sound cool; the goal is to bring yourself back to your loving nature and be a stronger and more spiritually empowered version of yourself. If you still find it difficult to shift your energy after speaking your mantra, try sitting with it and repeating it several times so you can feel into and resonate with it as much as possible. Imagine how you would feel if you indeed received that new direction and had clarity.

A very powerful spiritual practice that you can do anytime is engaging in moment-to-moment prayer. Whenever you see yourself falling into fear, no matter where you are, call for backup. Ask for help. It really is as simple as it sounds. You may not always be able to shift your thinking because of how you feel in the present moment, but there is another way. Ask the same power that created you and keeps you thinking to shift your perspective for you. That's right. Acknowledge that you've detoured from intention, accept that your best mind is what brought you here, and then invite in a new way to see life. I often use the prayer, "God, I let go and let You guide me. Please allow my eyes to see with love."

Often when I get to my front door, I stop and say a prayer before I walk in. I release all the negativity I may have picked up throughout my day and ask for help to stay connected to my healthy, loving spirit as I walk into my home to see my wife and children. I can't tell you how many times I have felt and experienced Divine guidance in those moments. Prayer is a powerful medium for practicing surrender. It is a bridge that helps you let go of your controlling, fear-based mind and enter the enlightened, infinite mind of a loving presence.

Sometimes, though, it's hard to stop and have this inner dialogue. In these moments, I find that simply returning to my breath is all I need and often all I can do. God breathed life into humankind, and it is through breath that we continue to live. There is a lot of power in returning to a conscious breath. Right now, take a moment to take a deep breath in through your nose, then slowly let it out through your mouth.

Now, again, once more. In through your nose, then let it out slowly through your mouth.

Can you feel yourself relax and sink deeper into the present moment from the conscious breath? Being fully present with the inhalation and exhalation can be an entire experience. By the end of it, you may have enough presence to shift your way of thinking.

The goal of reciting a mantra, saying a quick prayer, or taking a conscious breath is to be present enough to stop the flow of ego, the need to control everything that's happening in your life, and to create enough inner space for the real you to shine through. This is how you return to clarity and step into living life with intention. Trust yourself and trust the process. It doesn't happen overnight, but the more you practice, the more you'll experience the peace of your presence.

Remember to be mindful of how you are feeling. When I feel happy, I believe that all is well in the world and that I am good and able. Your feelings are indicators of what you are believing. You feel what you believe. This whole practice is an art of noticing. When you notice you are slipping, call it out. Name it to tame it. Remind yourself that you are thinking this way and release it. You can make a decision today to commit to a different way of thinking. Reset your intention to what you crave more than anything else in the world: to feel good in your true nature. You can always ask for Divine assistance and invite a loving mindset to enter and replace your fear-based one.

Focus on Purpose

This is the point where you and your intentions meet. It's all about living your life as if you're choosing everything you're doing on purpose instead of being reactive to what life throws at you. This is a choice to consciously be who you want to be as often as possible.

You are made in the image of the Creator, so that means you have the power to be the creator of your life. Somewhere along the way, we stopped creating and became managers of our circumstances. We spend our time putting out little fires instead of igniting the powerful fire within ourselves. When we can let go of everyone else's opinions and all the limiting beliefs and fears that we carry, we can rise up and live with the true intention of life, which is to be an expression of the Creator.

Here are three ways to shift the direction of your attention:

- **Soul focus:** remembering who you are here to be

- **Purpose focus:** remembering what you are here to do

- **Solution focus:** remembering how you want to look at your life situation

Soul focus: When you live with intention, you don't dwell on who you are on the outside; rather, you focus on the inner nature of who you really are. You are a soul in a body, not a body with a soul. Do you see yourself as this temporary, finite body or as an eternal being traversing this life?

Remind yourself of what, deep down, resonates as true. In your mind or out loud, affirm to yourself, "I am part of the Infinite. I am a powerful part of the Creator. I am strong. I am loving, kind, and perfect as I was created. I have infinite patience. I am eternal. I am forever. I am abundant, I am energy, I am bigger than this body. I am bigger than my life situation. I don't care what others think of me. I live on purpose."

Whether it's emotional disharmony or a bad habit, as often as possible, focus on the reality that this isn't really you. It is just an outer layer, like the skin of a lizard you will shed in time. Your essence shines bright and doesn't have imperfections. Frame your imperfections as part of your earthly mission, knowing full well that they have been given to you for a reason.

By shifting your focus to your connection to infinite power and unlimited potential, you can get others' opinions out of your head. Who cares what your neighbor thinks? Any judgment from somebody else is just an immature assessment of the outermost layer of who you are. They are judging the shoe! Would you ever judge somebody's character and value based on their shoe? You can let go of what people think about you when you realize that they aren't looking at the real thing anyway.

Furthermore, when you start focusing on the souls of others, you can also stop judging them. Comparison, competition, and jealousy exist only on the outer layer. When you shift to your soul focus, you accept that whatever is happening on the outside is just the way another person is wired and that they have been given a totally different mission than you. You can choose to send love and blessings to them as they go through life and become a silent ally for them in their struggles.

Purpose focus: When you live with intention, you don't dwell on what you have to do; you focus on what you want to do. Ask yourself the following: What inspires you? What makes you come alive? What makes you feel free? What are your passions? What are your dreams? If you could do anything, what would you do? If you could travel anywhere, where would you go? If you could be with any kind of person, whom would you be with?

Dreams are soul food, and if you want to live, you have to eat. If you love sports, play. If you love hiking, climb. If you love the beach, hit the sand. If you need a break, take one! You have to create time to do the things you love if you want to love the life you live. This applies to your career as well. I am not saying you should quit your job right now, but if you don't love what you do, it's time to start thinking about what you would do if you could do anything. Dream about it. If you don't have a job, focus on what you would like to do if you could get one tomorrow. Your job isn't to say *how*, your job is to say *yes*.

Take action toward what you love, even if it's small. When you are inspired by something, make a move, no matter how big or small. The Universe rewards small steps in the right direction. In fact, you will notice that work stops feeling like work, starts being fun, and becomes a joy in your life. When I was training for a marathon, I was blessed to work with an incredible coach, Herve. He spoke with a French accent and was always filled with amazing information and encouragement.

One day after our training session, I turned to Herve and asked, "Do you do anything else besides train runners?"

He smiled and said, "No."

"That must be pretty awesome, right?"

He looked me in the eyes and said, "I don't work. I have fun. I do what I love, and I get paid for it. Yes, it's pretty awesome."

We all have a calling. Whether that's being a stay-at-home mom, a plumber, an architect, or a lawyer, when you find the love in what you do, you'll never have to *work* another day in your life. You are already worthy of living the life you want to live.

Solution focus: When you live with intention, you don't dwell on your problems. Focusing on your problems is another way of focusing on your powerlessness. The twelve-step community uses the power of the Serenity Prayer: "God, grant me the serenity to accept the things I cannot change, the courage to change the things I can, and the wisdom to know the difference." Sure, there are things you truly cannot change, but if you believe you are a part of the unlimited power and potential of your Source; that you have within you a storehouse of infinite patience, joy, energy, abundance, and kindness; and that you were placed in this world with a mission and a calling, then please focus on your courage to change the things you can.

I once attended a lecture by author and motivational speaker Alon Ulman, and at a certain point in the talk, he said something that still resonates with me today. He looked at the crowd and said, "You have to stop looking at your problems and complaining about their difficulty, why they are holding you back, and whether or not you should continue. If you believe in your mission, always ask yourself, 'How can I? How can I? How "yes"? How "yes"?' Don't discuss why this could fail; don't focus on 'no.' Shift your focus to 'How "yes"?' Success isn't determined by resources but by being resourceful."

What you think about expands. Dwelling on what's going wrong sends a message out into the Universe that you are connected to that thing, so more of it will come your way. When you shift your focus to solutions, even if you don't actually have a solution, you are in a position of spiritual power. Genuine focus on solutions will attract insight and wisdom that you can use to move forward. When you are solution-focused, you feel energetically good and positive, which allows you to think more clearly and react as an empowered individual rather than a victim of your circumstances. It feels like hope.

Focus on where things are going right, and more things will go right. Instead of focusing on why it won't work, focus on why it will.

Play Make-Believe

My parents and I were walking together one afternoon, and I was expressing my painful experience of trying to get some well-known figures in the world of spirituality to endorse my first book. For me, the process was full of false promises at best and a total lack of response at worst. I was totally out of alignment, and my emotions were getting the best of me.

My father looked at me and gently said, "Moshe, you have to act as if."

I said, "Dad, I don't really get what you're trying to say."

He repeated himself: "Act as if. You have to act as if you already have all the endorsements you want."

My mother chimed in, "Yes, Moshe, as long as you're in this negative headspace, you're blocking anything from coming in."

Though I was aware of this concept, this was the first time I'd heard it in a way that penetrated my being. *Right! Act as if!* I thought. After that moment, I totally changed my attitude and shifted the way I was talking about the book and the endorsements. Over the next few weeks, I spoke in brighter tones, walked taller, and acted as if I had everything I needed in place and was just waiting for the blurbs to show up in my inbox. And you know what happened? They did.

There is an awesome power in acting as if you already are the person you want to be and have achieved the things you want to achieve. *Feel it to reveal it.* It's not about faking anything; it's about playing make-believe, like we did as children. It's using your imagination, feeling into the experience, and stepping into wonderland. When you act as if, you are not "faking" it because you are actually living closer to the truth of who you are. When you feel good and positive and are thinking, speaking, and acting as if you just won the lottery of life, your life will undoubtedly begin to shift.

I challenge you to write down what your life would look like if everything went the way you'd like it to go. What would your personality be like, how would you feel, where would you live, what car would you drive, what would your career be, what would you be doing in your leisure time, and in what way would you be contributing to your community? Start with these questions as a baseline and then further explore who you would want to be in your ideal life. Be as detailed as possible and describe a picture of who you would love to be and the life you would want to have.

Sometimes when I share this in a live workshop, I feel waves of panic emanating from the participants. People feel that they have to decide their entire future at that moment, and they fear they'll get it wrong. Don't be nervous or feel that there is any pressure in this exercise. You are not married to your answers. You can always do this again in the future, and it can be something fun and exciting and different each time. And remember, throughout your life, you really always want the same thing. It just takes different forms.

Feeling good is the prayer behind your prayers and desire behind your desires. Whatever form your desire takes, there is one clear underlying, motivating desire: the belief that with the achievement of this desire, you will feel good. Everything you want, you want because you believe you will feel good in having it.

Once you have clearly created a picture of the ideal you, I challenge you to take this one step further and act as if it were already true. For the rest of the day, walk, talk, and breathe as if you are the person on that page. Feel the feelings of being that person, and make this a fun experiment. In addition, I suggest trying to recognize any resistance to this. When you feel the cynical part of you say, "This is dumb. I don't know why I am doing this" or "This won't work. Why on earth would this work?" or "I can't actually act this way. People will think I am crazy," remind yourself that this is the voice of fear trying to stop you from feeling the good feelings of your imagination. It's just one day. Try it and see what happens. If it's fun and you enjoy it, try it again tomorrow. If it was hard for you, try probing and asking yourself why it was so hard for you and see if you gain insight into your character in the process. God imagined the world into reality; you can too. *Feel it to reveal it.*

A question I suggest you become used to asking yourself is "Is this leading me toward or away from my ideal self?" If you want to truly be happy for the rest of your life, commit to being you. Commit to feeling good. Don't be more afraid of living than you are of dying. As children, we are afraid of the dark; as adults, we're more afraid of the light.

Focus Less on What You Want to Do and More on Who You Want to Be

On my second date with my wife, we met at the Inbal Hotel lobby café in Jerusalem. Pretty early in the conversation, she asked me about my dreams and aspirations. "What do you want to do when you get older?" I remember clearly thinking for a moment and saying, "I am not 100 percent sure what I want to do. But I'm focused less on what I want to do and more on who I want to be."

The only real way to experience the joy of your life is to embrace yourself fully. You were created with certain gifts, talents, and abilities. Use them. When you use the gifts you were created with, you experience more of your Creator. You have ideas about life and how you want to live, so live them. Today is truly the first day of the rest of your life. Set your intention to the tune of "I am going to do whatever I need to do to fully live as my true Self today."

Abraham was a man on a mission to find God, and when he finally made contact, the first thing God told him was essentially "If you want to find me, go find yourself. You can't find me anywhere else." The rest of the original verse says, "Go to yourself, [and leave] your land, your birthplace, and your father's home, to a land which I will show you."[2] First of all, for an all-knowing God, this verse seems really out of order. Logically, you first have to leave your house before you can leave your city, and this must all happen before you can leave your country. Rather, God is telling you that conceptually, you first have to leave the thoughts, beliefs, and opinions of your social systems, beginning with the overarching culture of the country you live in and then, more specifically, your city and immediate social circle. Only then can you make the biggest leap, which is stepping away from the thoughts and beliefs you've held on to from childhood, which you received in your parents' home. You have to wake up to the fact that your country, social network, and parents simply don't and never did have all the answers. And that's not just OK; that's exactly the journey! God didn't even tell Abraham where to go but rather said, "Go to a land which I will show you." Why? Because if God were to tell him exactly where to go, God would be no different than his parents. The answers have to come from within, not from outside. Otherwise, you'll never really find yourself. In fact, the words themselves read "to a land which I will show you," which means not just "I will show you the place where you need to go" but also "I will reveal to you the truth of who you are."

There is a Proverb that says, "One must walk in their own straightness."[3] What does this mean? It means that you need to walk in line with the Truth that is your own. Your life has to resonate. Your life has to make sense to you. Your fear story is keeping you back from fully embracing yourself. Drop that old story. Remember your dream. Live in alignment with who you are meant to be.

This is an inner commitment that you don't need to tell anybody about, and I strongly urge you to carefully consider whom you share this with in the beginning of your practice. To anyone who is not yet ready to be free, this may trigger the fear within them, causing them to mock the idea of living a love-filled life. There will come a time when everyone around you will be so moved by your presence that you won't need to tell anyone; they will be coming up and asking you how you made such a positive, radical shift.

Regardless, on your way toward personal freedom, don't let anyone who laughs at your spiritual growth make you feel embarrassed. There will always be naysayers, people who mock what you are trying to do and simply don't understand. Forgive them for this because this is simply where they are in their spiritual evolution. Send them silent blessings and thanks for reminding you of how lucky you are to be at your stage in awakening.

We're all on our own journey. You can only take responsibility for yourself. Be confident in your decision to focus on authenticity. It takes courage to choose yourself, and you will likely make mistakes, but you won't regret it. I certainly made, and continue to make, many mistakes along the way. I don't let those mistakes deter me, though. Learn from your mistakes because that's what they are there for. They are part of the Divine lessons we're here to learn. The great ones fall many times and get back up. On the simplest level, what separates them from the rest is not that they fall; it's that they are willing to accept that falling is part of the process and just dust themselves off and get back up. I have learned to do this, and I'm sure you can do it too. On a deeper level, it's the falling itself that makes us great. So fail fast, fail often, and then get up and learn from it for the future. When you take out risk, you take out opportunity. You become what you practice most, so become someone who turns fear into love at all costs.

Listen to your inner voice that knows the truth, and don't let fear drive your life anymore. What people think about you is less important than what *you* think about you. And what you think about you is less important than what you actually are. Remember the shoe called you. Don't get caught in the shoe. There is an immeasurable and eternal you who knows and loves and is more perfect, beautiful, and kind than you can ever imagine. Be the channel for your creative genius, and freely live your life with intention. Freedom doesn't mean you're able to do whatever you want to do. It means you're able to fully be who you are. So go to yourself. Go for yourself. It may sound like an ego-driven desire, like "I am going to go do this for me. I am going toward me." But the Truth is going toward your true Self isn't ego. Your ego is what's keeping you from taking the leap.

Shift your intention for living with an "I have to do" mindset to a "What I want to be is everything" mindset. Intend to return. Intend to feel happy. Intend to feel good. Intend to be exactly who you're meant to be. To live with intention is to light up your inner fireplace, the place of your inner fire. A fireplace warms up the inside of a home, no matter how cold it is outside. You have to light and fan your fire so it won't matter anymore how cold it gets outside you.

In the next chapter, we'll discuss the condition of certainty. In clarifying a new belief about how life works, this will help you drop the fear-based agreements you've made with life. It will help you choose yourself and not feel guilty about it. Knowing that the world is working to your benefit and that you are always moving in the right direction will give you comfort in the process and the strength to get up and keep going when you've fallen down. I am excited to share this next step with you.

CHAPTER FOUR

The Condition of Certainty

Be Certain in the Presence of Love

I love the condition of certainty, and I am sure you will too. It might be the single most important principle you could ever live with, and it stands at the core of spiritual enlightenment.

When I say *certainty*, I mean an absolute clarity that everything is right and good, as it is right now. That life is unfolding exactly how it is supposed to, with a divine intent to bring you and all of life toward the experience of the highest good. Not ever making an enemy out of the present moment but befriending it exactly as it is. Certainty is knowing that everything that you experience today, everything that has happened in your past, and all that will happen in your future are guiding you toward the best possible outcome for you. It is trusting that you are in good hands, being taken care of, and being tended to. It is being certain about the presence of love, the presence of God. It is faith in a divine Infinite Intelligence that is organizing, handling, and managing everything in your life. It is knowing that there is a force that desires your partnership as well as your health, creativity, goodness, expansion, and joy. In short, certainty means feeling that all is well, everything is working out, and things are getting better.

I have personally had the blessing of being raised by parents who didn't just talk the talk but walked the walk with this principle, and it created the baseline for all of my spiritual growth. They raised me and my brothers with a deep knowing that everything in our lives was OK. In fact, things were better than OK; they were always working out perfectly. Before the days of GPS, we would get lost driving somewhere, and my mother would always say, "How fun is this! Let's see what's going to happen next." No matter what happened, my parents were certain that our circumstances were purposeful, good, and direct guidance from something Higher.

I know that for some, this may literally be a leap of faith, but what I suggest is that for the rest of this chapter, suspend any disbeliefs you may have and give living with certainty a chance. You may be surprised to find a way of living that is deeper, calmer, more joyful, and more full of love than the one you were handed. The more you experience the positive results of living with certainty, the more certain you will become.

Certainty is a premise for living. This is what gets you through the "what ifs" of the future, the "how comes" of the past, and the "what nows" of the present. When you live with the faith that everything that happens is not a coincidence and that nothing is ever random, your world changes and your whole life takes on new meaning. You start paying attention to the details and listening for the messages in the wind. There is guidance everywhere, and the more you open yourself up to it, the more you'll experience synchronicity in everything you do, everyone you're with, and everywhere you go.

I want you to become doubtless about this. It is actually possible to go through life trusting without any doubt that there is a divine organization to life, that everything has been set up with perfect loving intention, and that it continues to unfold that way, leading you toward your purposeful highest good and a loving outcome. In this trust is a knowing that you are being guided and directed and that whatever you are experiencing is purposeful. Realize that there are no mistakes. There are no accidents. There are no isolated events, and nothing is random. If you happen to arrive at your meeting early, that is on purpose. If you see a number, image, or phrase over and over again in a way that you might normally just call a coincidence, there is something hidden there for you. It's all connected, and it's all for you.

Three Senses of Certainty

Let's take a step back and remember what we are doing here. Our work in life is the work of remembering that we are not just physical beings. Remembering who we are beyond our name, address, and occupation. Remembering that we are connected to everything and everyone and are all part of the infinite Oneness that is reality.

So, then, what are we doing here if we're really spiritual beings? Life is a journey of spiritual development. During our childhood, and to varying degrees, most of us have shifted out of harmony with our soul, and the life we lead is all about realigning and getting back in touch with that deeper truth. We came here with something to learn and something to teach. We all have something to gain and something to offer. The greatest teachers throughout history have taught us that at the core of all teachings is the fact that love is king. Thus, life is really a divine method of education. In this sense, you are a student in the cosmic classroom at the school of love. True Love is a language we're not innately fluent in, and we must spend the majority of our lives learning how to speak it. This is what the ancients meant when they said we are here to know God. We are not here to learn *about* God; rather, we are here to *know* God, to experience the love that is divine and become more Godly in the process.

Charles, a very close friend of mine, likes to say that although most people are focused on changing from being good to being great, the real goal of life is to go from being great to being truly good. To know love is to awaken, to come closer to consciousness and experience what life is all about. This is the universal energy of all things.

At any given moment, there are two parts to your life. There is what's happening on the inside and what's happening on the outside.

When I talk about your life's purpose, these two aspects are present. There is an inner purpose and an outer purpose. In other words, there is who you are here to be and what you are here to do.

Everyone has the same inner purpose: experiencing the true depth of who you are. The awareness of your *being* and the Source of all being is at the heart of living a life fulfilled. This is what many have called enlightenment. In Chasidus, it is called *deveikut*, which means "a unified connection with the Infinite." It has been called Nirvana, the Kingdom of Heaven, and today, many refer to it as engaging with consciousness, stillness, or awakening. It really doesn't matter what you call it. What matters is that you experience it and know it from the inside. This knowing is not an idea in your head but a full sensory experience. It affects how you perceive reality, how you feel, and ultimately how you behave. It is a way of life. It is a way of peace, joy, and love.

Every person's outer purpose differs from another's. No two people are here to do the same thing and have the same experiences. We all play different roles and have different functions throughout our lives. We play as children, then as adolescents, then as adults. We are daughters and sons, brothers and sisters, mothers and fathers, friends, coworkers, employees, citizens, political party members, and so on. Each person's part is different, not better or worse. The role you play is simply that: a role. It doesn't say anything about the essence of who you are. It only defines what you do and where you fit into the outer picture.

Now, I will specifically use the word *sense* because certainty is something that is beyond your analytical mind. You can sense deep within yourself that something is true. Even though you can't empirically show me this power or hand me this force, I can still experience an inner knowing, a sense of its truth, that is beyond logic and rationale.

Let me introduce you to the three senses of certainty:

1. **Certainty about the loving past:** The first sense is intuitively knowing that everything you have ever experienced is the perfect setup for your life's mission, tailor-made with perfect, loving intention. That means both *who* you are supposed to be and *what* you are supposed to do. Know that the family you're born into, the place you're from, the language you speak, and the society you grew up in are all on purpose. What you have and what you don't are helping you get exactly where you need to be to learn the lessons on your journey. This includes your challenges, your setbacks, and the divinely orchestrated detours. Everything is and has been for you and your personal evolution.

2. **Certainty about the loving present:** Next is sensing that you are part of a co-creation with the Infinite, which wants you to thrive and be the best possible version of yourself, dream big, and know that guidance, assistance, and support can and will be brought to you, no matter what you deeply desire. Sometimes the most important opportunities in your life slip in the back door through what appears to be a seeming misfortune or defeat. If you fail to recognize it, you may not pick up on what it's doing for you. Sometimes your ticket to success will come in a different form or from a different direction than you were expecting. God wants more for you than you could ever want for yourself, so even when it doesn't feel like it, that's when you have to remember that everything is really working for you. It's your daily choice to lean into a vision of love and a supporting Universe or into fear and doubt that you are doing this alone. Life is helping you come closer to knowing the truth of who you are, moving you on to the next stage in your spiritual development. Life is always working in your favor.

3. **Certainty about the loving future:** Finally, the third is sensing that there are infinite, limitless potential and possibilities and that they want your partnership. Recognize that anything can happen in any number of ways. To the same degree that God wants you to dream, God wants to bring your dreams to life. This trust includes having the patience to wait for your dreams to manifest in the right way and at the right time and the humility to know that there is a bigger and better vision of your life than you can ever imagine, and therefore your Source will always provide what you desire unless something better for you is waiting in its place.

When you're certain about your life, you live every day in love. A well-known Chasidic teaching is that you know you are living in love when the most important thing in your life is your desire to be connected to this loving Source. In the book of Psalms, King David says that his closeness to God, to this loving energy, is not just a good thing but rather is the definition of good. I know that everything flows better when I am aligned and plugged in to this force. I may not always feel ecstatic, but there is an inner knowing that whatever I have to do to be plugged in and connected to the unified loving energy of the world is the most important thing I can do at any given moment.

We nurture this connection through meditation and prayer, spiritual teachings, and acts of kindness. When you tune in to the channel of this divine love, you draw new energy and vivify your life's purpose as you connect with it. In the light of certainty, it doesn't matter what's going on in your life situation because your *life* is filled with the energy of this connection. You can, therefore, weather the storms and take advantage of the clear skies.

It doesn't mean that if you are certain about a particular outcome that you will certainly attain it, but it does mean you can see whatever happens as something that is unfolding in the highest order for your highest good. It is through this lens that you realize that life isn't happening *to* you; it is happening *for* you.

It Doesn't Just Feel Good to Feel Good; Feeling Good Is Positive Action

Remember the BRANCHes of the miracle mindset from chapter 1? I want to take some time now to focus on the branch of attraction, which is really part of something much bigger. It's what we call divine providence or divine interference. In addition to experiencing the joy and clarity that come with the miracle mindset, you will find that your feelings actually effect change in the world. A verse in the book of Proverbs says, "As the face is reflected in the water, so too does the heart of man."[1] We live in a world of reflection. The world will always reflect your heart back to you, meaning what you feel is what you'll find. What you feel is what will be shown to you. The more you lean into the trust of certainty, the more you'll start to experience synchronicity, receive crystal-clear messages and guidance, and actively rely on this power to work with you in manifesting your desires or something even better.

Why do these reflective changes take place? Because the Universe is set up in such a way that the vibrational energy we put out is what we receive. What we attract into our life is a response to how we feel, and how we feel is a response to what we truly believe. So in essence, what you believe is ultimately what you'll receive. The Universe responds to your energy, not your words. Your words may shift the energy you're sending out, but what's far more important is the feeling behind the words. Feeling good is actually a constructive act. Let's look at each of the three main aspects of divine intervention.

Synchronicity: Synchronicity is a divine mode of communication. Have you ever heard your phone ring and before you even looked at it, you just had a feeling about who it was? Have you ever been working hard on a project and the information you needed just wound up on your desk? Have you ever needed a break and then, through some turn of events, got a random day off? These are all examples of synchronicity. It can be easy to think of them as coincidences, but the truth is there are no coincidences because the world happens on purpose. When you experience synchronicity, it's because you are in sync with reality. You are living in alignment and are harmonizing with the divine intention of life. On the other hand, when you don't experience synchronicity, it means you're not in spiritual alignment with the Universe.

The Universe is aware of your thoughts, your words, and certainly your actions. Nothing is hidden, and everything receives a response. You can't think a thought that doesn't create a shift on some level, nor can you speak without it causing another thought. When you are in rapport with the Infinite, It expresses itself back to you. These are the winks from behind the veil.

The more you lean into the certainty of the Infinite Divine Intelligence that manages even the smallest things in your life, the more synchronicity you'll start to experience. Sometimes the divine providence is so clear and so removed from the normal cycle of things that these things literally feel like miracles. And the truth is they are. Every single synchronistic experience is a little miracle happening loudly enough for you to hear where it's coming from. Nothing in this world is natural. Everything is a miracle. The only difference between a miracle and nature is our perception, as we tend to experience nature as a continual common occurrence.

Guidance: When you are certain that you are being guided and helped along the way, clear guidance will be presented to you more often. Sometimes it's simply an intuitive feeling, a knowing where you need to go, what you need to do, or that you are in exactly the right place. Other times there is a lightning bolt of clarity or an insight that comes from a place you can't explain. Often signs can start showing up in your daily life, for example, in a text message, in a blog you read, in a song on your playlist, or on the side of a truck on the highway. When you start paying attention to the messages, you'll start to notice that divine direction is following you everywhere you go. Intuition is guidance from within. Apparent coincidences and signs are guidance from without. To deny this is to deny life, for God is life in action, manifesting in every moment as who you're with, what is happening, and all that you perceive.

Once I was finishing a lecture at a seminar, and one of the logistics coordinators came over to me after the event and said, "Isn't it hard for you to have a one-way conversation?"

I said, "Joe, I don't understand what you mean. Could you please clarify?"

He looked straight in my eyes and said, "Moshe, is it not hard for you to believe in a God that doesn't talk back?" I was shocked. This was a man who I knew was a person of strong faith, and that was the day I learned that even people who believe in a higher power don't always live in complete communication with spirit.

I said, "I don't know about your God, but mine definitely responds, often very quickly and always with a loving smile, whether I like what was said or not."

Another way to think about the unfolding of your life is to see the Universe as a world-class coach. When you hire a good coach, you know you're always getting the best advice, guidance, and direction. Often you may be required to do some hard work, but it is always with a purpose, for your own good, and to help you get where you really want to be. That is exactly how life works. You now have access to the best coach that has ever existed. Enjoy it, lean on it, and have fun in the process.

Manifesting: One of the most empowering experiences is knowing that you are in a partnership with the Universe and that you can co-create your life experience by changing the way you think about life and the way you feel about situations. Whether you call it the law of attraction, the secret, or the power of intention, your ability to create your reality is real.

You don't manifest what you want; you manifest who you are. Everywhere you go, you broadcast who you are. What you broadcast is what you're tuned in to. What you're tuned in to is what you receive. The more you lean into life with the certainty of this loving connection, the more you prime yourself to be an energy magnet for all things of that nature. This is the aspect of certainty that is all about knowing that God wants more for you than you could ever want for yourself and that you have the power to attract the things you want into your life. It's trusting that you are powerful and being certain that you have a senior partner who is there the whole time, assisting you in getting where you want to be. The Universe works fast when you're open and ready.

This actually brings us back to the condition of intention. We already spoke about living your life with the intention of being fully you. When you embrace certainty, you not only intend to live your life as your authentic self but also know that whatever is happening in your life is helping you do so. Life accepts you as you are. When you do the same, you start supercharging yourself for miracles in everything you do.

There have been many times in my life when what I thought was a problem actually turned out to be awesome guidance and ultimately a true blessing. I spent a good number of years deeply engrossed in study before I decided I was ready to seriously start dating. I didn't have any plans to jump in until I felt settled with what I was doing and where I was going. One afternoon, I received a phone call from a good friend about a woman who was just "perfect" for me. I thanked him but told him I wasn't dating.

Not more than a few hours later, I got a call from a totally different acquaintance who said the same thing. I was curious, and when I asked the person's name, it was the same woman. I still answered that I was not dating and would just have to see if she was still available when I was ready. Without exaggerating, I received five more phone calls within the next week from different people, all unrelated to each other but somehow connected to this woman.

Well, I guess you can figure out what I did next. I went out with her. *Seven* people in *seven* days! I was shocked at the weird synchronicity. I just knew she would be the one. And then . . . she wasn't. Our connection was short-lived. We dated for a couple weeks, but I spent most of my time trying to figure out what on earth had gotten into everyone I knew. There was nothing similar about us at all. A couple weeks of my life were caught up in weirdness, dates that seemed to go nowhere, and a group of people who made me question how well they knew me. My dating doors were closed for years, and all of a sudden they swung open because of these strange coinciding phone calls. At the time, I was pretty frustrated.

Almost immediately after I stopped dating this woman, I received a phone call from my mother saying, "Moshe, I found your wife." *Yeah, yeah, yeah. I've heard that before,* I thought. Nevertheless, I was somewhat open to it because, at that point, I had already put my feet in the water (and my mom is clairvoyant). This time, though, she was right. I met my wife, the woman of my dreams, the very next week. I would not have been open to it before going through that whole dating drama. I was too caught up in my own head and in developing my craft. The Universe had other plans, even if that meant frustrating me for a few weeks and getting seven different people to make a call about the wrong woman. I tell this story to say that even when it looks as if you're going the wrong way, you are always being guided. Remember that life isn't happening to you; it's happening for you.

In this chapter, we uncovered how powerful it can be to be certain in the loving presence of our past, present, and future and know that divine intervention and miracles are present with us as we go about our lives. In the next chapter, we'll look at what holds us back from living this way, what it looks like when we live in doubt instead of certainty, and how we can begin to shift out of disharmony and into a peaceful state of alignment.

CHAPTER FIVE

Applying Certainty—Living with Love Is an Active Choice

The Dream of Certainty or Nightmare of Doubt (FEAR)

L ife with intention and certainty is a dream. You feel positive, encouraged, and excited to see what the day brings you. The only problem is that much of the time, we choose to live in a nightmare. It's not our fault, though. We were programmed a certain way when we were children, and today, we have the opportunity to tap into the truth of reality and reprogram the way we experience our lives.

The opposite of certainty is doubt. Remember the Map. When we *believe* that love and success are uncertain, we think doubtful *thoughts* and experience *disharmony* in our life. When we shift out of a harmonious relationship with life, we fall into doubt, we have disharmonious thoughts, and we end up feeling and experiencing disharmony in our lives.

But sometimes I ask myself, *Why is it so hard to lean into love? Why is it challenging for us to look at the bright side when things are going wrong? Why do we walk around feeling anxious about the future and spend our precious time dwelling on the past?* The answer is the same thing that's holding us back from ourselves: FEAR. Once again, it is that false evidence appearing real that gets in the way of our living a life full of infinite, loving potential. We have inherited a fear story, a belief system that tells us the world is not supporting our doings, a system that believes we're the ones totally responsible for our lives and in total control of our circumstances. It's a belief system that preaches that, fundamentally, we are alone.

It's easy and totally natural to buy into the shell of the world. When we judge our life's circumstances based on a first glance or what happens on the outside, we end up with a very shallow perspective on life. Not only do we lose out on a deeper life, but we also carry this fear with us everywhere we go. The truth is, however, everything is going according to plan, and there is nothing to fear, even though it may not look or feel that way. When you shift your belief, bring your energy up to this higher Truth, and align yourself with the fact that you are being guided, your life will actually begin to unfold in an entirely different way.

Life is the work of remembering. When we spiritually forget and are unaware of this truth, we fall into all the negative patterns that hurt us and the people we're around. We complain, become frustrated, and create drama. We judge and criticize the people we spend time with and the events we experience. The more we step into and embrace certainty, the more we can experience the truth of what Franklin D. Roosevelt meant when he said, "The only thing we have to fear is fear itself." Fear is the great divider in our life. It separates and creates pain.

Superficially there are only three things that seem to have the power to sabotage your life plans: nature, other people, and yourself. Each of these presents another level of difficulty in leaning on the certainty of a loving presence in your life. It is much easier to see natural occurrences, such as a traffic jam, stormy weather, or dead batteries, as something guided by the divine. Our phrases may sound something like "Well, it is what it is. This is for the best. It's nobody's fault." We find it much harder, however, to not think judgmental thoughts when a person inflicts pain or makes a mistake. It's considered normal behavior to immediately judge how they've messed up, how they're wrong, and how you'd never do anything like that.

The secret is that you're meant to experience all of life, even when someone says or does something that hurts your feelings and is insensitive. Even when you're triggered by your mother or receive an email that upsets you, it's still all coming from the same source. It's still love. It's still good. It still has a lesson for you to learn. In addition, it is leading you to a higher and broader perspective than you had before the experience. This can be very difficult to put into practice, but when you lean into the certainty that you are always in loving hands, just as my child is certain that when I throw her up in the air, I will catch her, you will start to experience and learn the divine lessons that were tailor-made for you.

Typically, the hardest time to be certain is when you have caused pain or messed up. You take so much responsibility for your actions that you don't realize that even those things are expressions of love working through you. That in no way absolves you from repairing what you did, nor does it excuse laziness and apathy. Nevertheless, it's true. Even when you mess up, you were supposed to experience some form of temporary defeat so you could learn a lesson or, in some cases, teach one.

Doing and Being Done

This actually brings us back to the central block between us and the Infinite. A verse in Deuteronomy says, "And I stand in between you and God."[1] The Baal Shem Tov explains the verse as meaning that it is none other than you, the I, the ego, that stands in between the light of who you are and all the love of the Universe. Our belief that we are in control cuts us off from experiencing the light and love of God.

It is right in that moment, when you put all of your trust in your own power, that you experience fear. It is when you've forgotten you're part of something so much bigger and more real than your body, when you think you're totally in control, that you experience frustration. It is when you think that nobody but you can take care of this that you feel stress and anxiety. Ego is the process of Edging God Out. When we think we know the whole story of life, it creates this fear and ego that hold us back from our certainty. There is a fullness that leads to emptiness and an emptiness that leads to fullness. Emptying ourselves of our ego, our ego-driven desires and the illusion of time, leaves us feeling our natural sense of wholeness.

In the womb, you didn't do anything at all; you were being done. Nothing was left undone, and you were being completed in a state of total surrender. Then you were pushed out of there, and you basically said, "Thank you, God, I'll take it from here." Instead of being a piece of God, you decided to be something different. You started to believe that now you were in charge.

Stepping into the presence of the light is scary because you have to have faith that something will catch you. Remember the Proverb about water reflecting the face looking upon it, and the heart reflecting the same. When we think we're in total control, we live with resistance to anything that goes against what we want; we live with nonacceptance, which is a strong negative energy. Nonacceptance is like seeing an image in the mirror and not liking what you see, so you attack it. And guess what? It attacks you back. By this logic, that also means that if you fully accept it, the image will accept you back. If you make it your friend, it will befriend you. If you show it love and joy, it will show you love and joy. That is how you change your life. That is how you change the world.

It's time to break the mental agreements you have made with life and change the way you see things. Commit to unlearning the limitations of what the world taught you. When they told you that if you fail, you are a failure, it was a lie. When they said no pain, no gain, that was a lie. When they said you have to be wealthy or attractive to get what you want in life, that was a lie. When they said this world is all you have, so eat, drink, and be merry, it was a lie. When they said you're all alone and you're not being supported, that was a lie. When they said rely only on yourself to get things done, that was a lie. When they said you are solely responsible for your life, that was a lie.

The truth is you are always being supported. You are never alone. You are always being loved. You are always exactly where you are supposed to be. Life is unfolding the way it is supposed to.

You are responsible for making the best decisions you can make with the tools and mind you were given. You are not here to get everything right; you are here to get better at everything that is right. Life doesn't end after death. We are eternal beings who are part of something Eternal and Infinite.

You can never *be* a failure; you can only *experience* failure so you can learn how to be more successful. You don't have to be in pain to learn something new. Life can be fun. It's supposed to be. Life can be light, and it should be. Life can be awesome, and it really is! You don't need any prerequisites to call out to the Infinite and connect. It doesn't matter what you have or don't have in the bank. It doesn't matter what you look like or how much you weigh. It doesn't matter whom you know or who knows you. It doesn't matter how successful you are or how many times you've fallen. You are always one thought away from a miracle, one thought away from a breakthrough, one thought away from living the best day of the rest of your life. This is the Truth. This is the power you have been given. There is a part of us that thinks we are the ones doing everything when the truth is we are being done just as much as we're doing. This is the Truth. The major lesson of life is that although we have the power to co-create with the Universe, we're simply not in control.

There are two verses that, when read side by side, deliver a life-altering message. One verse says, "Choose life,"[2] and the other says, "You who connect to God are alive today,"[3] which means "Connecting to the ever-present loving energy of God is life." These verses teach us the secret to life: to make love our main choice on a moment-to-moment basis.

No Outcomes Are Yours, and All Outcomes Are Good

Oftentimes one of the great setbacks of embracing a supporting universe is not seeing immediate results that match our desired outcomes. Here is the trick: don't get caught up on outcomes. It's not that I don't want you to have great outcomes, but you must do what you can, surrender to the highest Good, and feel positive about the whole experience. In fact, it's letting go and stepping into that happy place that creates an energetic magnet to bring your desire (or something better!) toward you.

Remember that great opportunities often slip in the back door. Know that there is a plan greater than yours, and there is a solution of the highest good that may or may not be aligned with what you've currently envisioned. When you do your part and let go, expressing infinite patience, you are already living in the light that is the peace that comes with knowing all is well. Let go of control and embrace the flow. Everything is already going according to plan. Everything is right on schedule. You are meant to be right where you are. Everything is happening on purpose, even when you don't feel as if you are heading in the right direction or you have thoughts that don't align with who you want to be. You're never not on purpose. Sometimes the greatest struggles are just the wrapping paper for our greatest gifts. We just need to trust that there is a loving present inside and start to open up. No outcomes are yours. All outcomes are good. And you're exactly where you need to be.

Yes, you got a parking ticket, and yes, it was unfair. Yes, your hair dryer broke the day of the wedding, and yes, the power went out during the Super Bowl. You can get angry, upset, and down, or you can laugh. You can remember that this too is for the good. This too is working out for you. This is also a magical moment. This is actually a miracle designed specifically for you. Once you can do this and surrender to the flow of life, you give yourself permission to lean into life and ask yourself how you would like to act.

Symptoms of Alignment

Earlier, we discussed the importance of knowing your physical and energetic symptoms so you can know when you've fallen out of alignment. Sometimes that means noticing that your behavior isn't showing your best side. Sometimes the way you're talking or whom you're talking about reveals it, and sometimes it's your thinking.

Most often you can tell right away by how you feel. What's going on inside you right now? Are you feeling high or low energy, peaceful or frustrated, happy, down, or bored? Let's explore what recognizing these symptoms looks like.

Notice the difference in your lived experience. If something challenging happens in your life, that might look like the difference between complaining, venting, and pouting and speaking words of acceptance, understanding, and gratitude. If it comes through another person, are you blaming, gossiping, and being defensive or accepting, understanding, and forgiving? Are you cursing or finding silence? Are you calm and staying positive? Become sensitive to how you respond emotionally and energetically. Do you find yourself becoming sad, disappointed, frustrated, angry, anxious, or worried, or do you spend most of your time in a state of positivity and acceptance of the present moment? Are you energetically negative or positive? Lazy or energetic? Weak and tired or inspired and enthusiastic?

What are your go-to physical symptoms? What do you turn to when you want to take the edge off? Do you put something in your body? Do you distract yourself and get lost in some form of media, or do you do something more positive, like exercise, listen to music, or let your creativity flow? Do you raise your voice, or do you speak calmly? Do you retreat or retaliate? Turn inward or outward?

Self-awareness is vital to your spiritual development. But what now? Let's say you become very good at being conscious of your ego symptoms and knowing when you're out of harmony with what you know to be true. Now what? As one of his main teachings, the Baal Shem Tov provided a three-step process that generations of his students have used when they notice they've fallen out of alignment and their thinking is off. In Hebrew, this process is called *Havdala, Hachna'a, Hamtaka*, which means "separate, release, and sweeten." This process has the power to elevate any situation you find yourself in. You can turn yourself around by turning yourself over.

1. **Separate:** Step one is noticing and being conscious of your inner world. Be mindful of how you're feeling and what you are thinking. Recognize whether you're in alignment and in harmony with your higher Self. Just consciously noticing that you are in a place of feeling emotionally undone and out of control is already a huge step forward. In this step, you separate yourself from feeling, which is the first step in taking away its power. When you can see it there within you, you can't be trapped by it anymore. You don't see yourself as angry; rather, you see anger or angry thoughts inside yourself. You stop identifying with the negative emotion and see it as something that is taking space inside your body.

2. **Release:** Take away its power. Let it go. Accept where you are and what has happened. The thoughts and feelings you're having right now were created out of the best mind you had just before they showed up. You didn't know any better. If you did, you wouldn't be feeling this way. What you're experiencing is a formed habit you created a long time ago, and you don't yet know any other way. Forgive yourself for thinking these kinds of thoughts, feeling these feelings, and speaking this way, and remind yourself that this isn't the real you. These are like old clothes you've suddenly outgrown that you can take off and throw away. Release yourself from the guilt of feeling this way and take a step forward. Remember this isn't the truth of who you are.

3. **Sweeten:** Recognize the source of the thought, and call it by its name: fear. Realize that the fear story took over to keep you safe. It had good intentions because it wanted you to feel love and safety, but it isn't developed enough to realize that it is only causing more pain. Remember that every thought you have is either an extension of love or is desperately calling out for love. From a place

of compassion, forgive yourself for having this kind of thought and give yourself what you are really looking for: love. Invite the ever-present energy of love to enter your mind and reinterpret your life situation. Ask for guidance and assistance in seeing yourself and your circumstances through a lens of love.

This is a powerful exercise that I use all the time. Whether you use it as a prayer or to reset the way you think, it is one of the more powerful tools you can keep in your bag to help you transcend the small and narrow way of living and live a life that is truly expansive and amazing. The only things you'll need before these three steps are a willingness to choose happiness, a willingness to choose love, a willingness to choose yourself, and a desire to feel good again.

Your mind won't naturally go to these loving thoughts at first. In the beginning, you will have to make an effort to think this way. But trust me, if you master the art of transformation, you'll create a new version of how you see the world. You can see the world you want to see. Repetition is the mother of mastery, and you become what you practice most, so continue to practice loving thoughts, and in the process, you'll become one who sees a loving world.

Challenges Are Divine Assignments, Lessons, Opportunities, or Reminders in Disguise

But what about when things certainly seem to be moving in the wrong direction? What if things *aren't* working out? What about when you lose your job, get sick, miss the bus, or get a flat tire? What about when your spouse seems uninterested in you? What about when you feel your life has real problems?

By now, we all probably have a master's degree from the University of Hard Knocks. Life doesn't always show its cards right away, and challenges certainly do show up. Still, hard doesn't mean bad. Challenging doesn't mean wrong. And hurdles don't mean broken. They are all seemingly indirect ways of getting us to our desired destination. We're always receiving new lessons to learn, reminders of what's truly important, and opportunities that slip in through the back door that often appear as misfortune or temporary defeat. The Universe will always deliver exactly what you need for the next step in your personal evolution.

These challenges are really spiritual assignments. They show up to help us transition into the next stage of who we can become. If you show up for your spiritual assignments with a willingness to grow and heal, miracles will start showing up in your life. If you don't show up for your lesson today, it will show up for you tomorrow. If you don't choose your lesson today, it will choose you tomorrow.

In the same breath, let me make one thing super clear: I am not saying you should suppress your emotions. Just the opposite. You have to be real about what you are experiencing right now. That is what I mean when I say be present. Be mindful, and honor your feelings and pain as they are. If you can't accept the circumstance, ask yourself if you can accept the nonacceptance and pain you are feeling because of the circumstance. The moment you start to feel is the moment you start to heal. Allowing yourself to feel the pain is of the utmost importance so it doesn't turn into running away and numbing it or, even worse, dumping this negative energy on someone else.

When you are ready to step toward relief, plug yourself back in to some level of certainty. Return to love. Stop, take a deep breath, and remind yourself of this truth. Know that you are only ever sent a mission you are ready for. You have what it takes to see and reinterpret this with eyes of love. Accept that you can't avoid assignments. Anything you don't show up for will keep showing up for you until you resolve, heal, and learn the cosmic lesson. Understand that it has shown up for your personal healing and growth.

Sometimes the obstacles are there because it would actually be bad for you to get what you want. Sometimes the Universe is testing your courage and conviction and strengthening your passion and belief in what you are trying to accomplish. Sometimes it is there to open you up internally and help you face yourself where it hurts most so you can develop and grow.

You may never know the exact reason why you encounter a specific challenge, but you can know for sure that it is love bending in your cosmic favor. When we can embrace the shadow side of life, the darkness, then we can start mastering life. Every bit of this contrast gives you the opportunity to clarify exactly what it is that you desire and what's important to you.

Setbacks can either be a portal into a deeper connection with love, reminding you to turn inward and awaken, or they can drag you down deeper into a negative unconscious state. You don't get to choose what happens in your life. However, you do get to choose how you think about what happens. You do get to choose how you respond. See this as an opportunity to choose life and a perception of love.

Let's say someone makes a rude comment about the way you're dressed after you've spent a half hour getting yourself together. With one simple remark, you might be ready to throw in the towel for the whole day, but when these little things happen, they are seriously big gifts. You now get the opportunity to put on your new lenses with the knowledge that whatever is happening in your life is totally for your benefit. As you feel the frustration build up within you, see those feelings as an occasion to stop and witness that your energy is shifting, your thoughts are probably becoming defensive, and you're becoming upset. Now you have a chance to turn it over, to witness your feelings and realize that somewhere inside, you are afraid of something. Only when you can witness the fear can you turn it over to a Higher Power and trust in something more powerful and loving to change the way you're currently looking at things.

Maybe you're afraid that they're right, or you may feel powerless in the situation. Whatever the fear is, you now have the chance to surrender it. Let it go, and invite a loving perspective in. Send that person a silent blessing and thank them for being a creative force in your life. They helped you grow. They pointed you back in the right direction. They helped you turn inward to the loving presence you have, and now you are choosing to elevate yourself.

A number of years ago, my parents were on vacation. They came back from the beach one afternoon to find that their car had been broken into and many of their items, including their laptop, stolen. They looked at each other almost in disbelief. Then my father grabbed my mother's hands and started dancing. She looked at him and said, "What on earth are you doing?" He said, "I am dancing. We have to dance. That's all we can do." We can choose to dance regardless of what happened.

I often use this mantra, sometimes several times over, when I am triggered by an event, and it sends me back to the center:

I see you.

Thank you, my teachers.

Bless you, my teachers.

I remember.

Make Allies, Not Enemies

Resisting certainty causes suffering, worry, and anxiety. All the pain and suffering in the world are caused by this disconnect. It perpetuates fear and is the root of narrow-mindedness, the root of struggle. When you feel that you have to rely on your own power to be safe, you are in for trouble.

My two daughters were once sitting next to each other, having what sounded like a deep conversation. At the time, they were four and six and weren't aware that my wife was listening in. They had just gotten into a fight, and after a yelling match and some childish banter, my intellectual and philosophical older daughter, Chaviva, looked at her little sister and said, "Ahava, did you know that we chose our families before we came here?"

"Yes, I did," Ahava confidently responded. "But I didn't know that you'd be here!"

My wife and I spent the next few days laughing at those comments, but the truth is we often act the same way. We may believe everything has a reason, that life has meaning and purpose, and that we are all connected, but most of us probably wouldn't have signed up for this if it meant going through that, meeting him, working there, failing at this—and the list goes on.

The Talmud says that before anything is created, it accepts its role and desires to manifest in this physical reality to learn certain lessons and perform certain tasks. However, our conscious minds are disconnected from this deeper knowing, what Dr. Bruce Lipton and others have called our superconsciousness. In the language of spirituality, we call it our soul or spirit, and it is this spirit that knows the way and guides us along it in the process of our life. The importance of this idea is that we can lean more deeply into reality as life presents itself. When we live in resistance to what's happening in our lives, who we're with, or what we're doing, we build up resentment and negative emotional energy inside us. This way of living damages both our body and soul. When you live with certainty, you know that all things are good and are guiding you toward achieving your life's potential.

Try the following exercise and see what happens. No matter what is happening in your life, act as if you chose it. No matter whom you are with, act as if you chose to be with that person. No matter what you're doing, act as if you chose to do it. Maybe you chose it to learn how to walk away. Maybe you chose it to learn how to conquer a fear. Maybe you chose it for any number of reasons, but accept, embrace, and then make an empowered decision. Turn whatever is happening in your life into your friend and not your enemy.

Make this your mantra:

I make allies, not enemies.

In any circumstance, you only ever have three choices: accept it fully, leave and walk away, or change it. To simply stand against reality is insanity. In fact, the Talmud says that whenever a person sins and goes against themselves, it is only ever because a momentary spirit of insanity entered them. We tend to think that no matter what is happening, we are always responsible for "doing something about it," but that's not always the case.

We tend to also include situations that are totally out of our control and can't be changed. We woke up with the flu, there are two feet of snow, or the flight was canceled. This is what is meant in the Serenity Prayer when it says, "and the wisdom to know the difference." Some things we just can't change. But what do we do instead? We complain, we dread, we worry, and we do all sorts of internal gymnastics because there is a part of us that feels like we have to do something; otherwise something bad will happen or the problem will be our fault. Well, the truth is sometimes there is nothing you can do and nowhere you can go. In those cases, leaning into the situation is the only way to prevent self-imposed suffering.

I too had to figure out how to stop punishing myself. That meant letting go of habitual thinking patterns and stepping into the light that was waiting for me. I had to ask myself, *What is holding me back from embracing this truth? Why am I denying the power of love?*

It took me time to pinpoint the root causes of my fear, but in the end, it's not about identifying the actual reason *why* we fear. It's about realizing that fear is what we're believing in and responding with. We can change that today by dropping fear and embracing a loving mindset instead.

Life Is Abundant, Eternal, and a Partnership

There are three realities that, when we become conscious of them, can change our whole lives and help them take on new meaning. The Maggid of Mezritch, the primary disciple of the Baal Shem Tov and one of the founders of the Chasidic movement, explains that the following three cognitive shifts brought Abraham to God consciousness.

Life is abundant: Abraham understood that the Universe is not lacking; it is abundant. There is an infinite source of whatever we could possibly need, and life is always working for you. When I say "life is abundant," I mean that it's not here today and gone tomorrow; rather, it's here today and *more* tomorrow. It's like sitting at a table with seven other people and the pie is finally served for dessert; it's the certainty and knowing that each person who takes a slice isn't taking your slice because there is always enough.

Shifting out of a scarcity mentality in which you think there is never enough—and therefore have to do whatever you can to take care of yourself—allows you to embrace the knowledge that the world is abundant in every area, be it health, wealth, relationships, clarity, well-being, inner peace, or spiritual connection. There is always enough. We are all being taken care of. Things are good and OK right now. That means you can surrender your ego to a Higher Power, knowing that the Universe will take care of you. You will get whatever you need for your life's unique journey and purpose. What you have is what you need, and what you don't have, you don't need. Life is supportive. Life is good. Life is abundant.

Life is eternal: The next layer of understanding is knowing that life doesn't end after death, knowing that you will live on beyond this physical plane. Therefore, if there is abundance in this world, there must be infinite and eternal abundance in a world beyond this physical plane. We are on this journey toward a higher good greater than we can even imagine. There is eternal meaning and purpose to what we are doing here, and we will experience even greater love after this life.

Life is a partnership: Co-creation: that is our journey. This is the big *aha* moment for Abraham when he realizes that not only is the world abundant and we are working toward an everlasting love, but we ourselves are part of this loving force. We have the opportunity to choose love at every moment. We can choose life. Choose to collaborate with the loving force of the world and *be* the good for God. You are an instrument of love. You are an instrument of peace. You are an instrument of goodness. There is no greater experience than being Godly.

The rewards of certainty are inner peace, happiness, mental clarity, and confidence. The peace of feeling taken care of and being in good hands. Your body somehow feels lighter. You carry a deep sense of belonging. Life seems to flow easily, and serendipitous events happen all around you. With this peace, you're not stressed out, anxious, or upset, and you have access to creative thinking and insights that you couldn't have reached without it. You experience an inner strength and confidence to unapologetically be true to yourself, to live with intention. With this knowing, you end the fear cycle. You live with trust that everything is fine right now and is moving in the right direction.

This awareness allows you to deeply accept life's circumstances, to be conscious that things are working out exactly as planned. This won't make all life situations easy, but it will make them acceptable. Get excited about what will happen next. Be curious about life instead of anxious about it. You can even become enthusiastic about life and its challenges when you realize that life is good for you.

The lowest level of enlightenment is hindsight. Oftentimes you can look back at a situation and know that everything was supposed to happen for the reason that was ultimately revealed. Certainty turns hindsight into the foresightful knowledge that everything is leading you in the right direction. Even setbacks, defeats, and tragedies are part of this whole unified system of education. It is all an expression of a bigger love—a love so big that we simply can't understand everything in the moment. We can't be happy about everything that happens. We simply can't perceive the good in every dark experience, but in the end we'll know that everything was, is, and will be part of the highest good possible. Miracles aren't seen in the dark; they're seen in the light. In the light of your positive perspective, you will begin to see life's circumstances as no less than miraculous.

Nurturing your certainty may be the most important aspect of your spiritual practice. Anytime you feel that something else is more important, it is probably your ego. Fear causes us to focus on things of less importance because when we fear, we lack the trust that things are working out when we choose to be true to ourselves. Choose being true to love.

Despite my years of practice, I still fall. I definitely still forget. It happens all the time. Alignment is not a certificate you get and then hang up on your wall. It is an ongoing process of awakening. The greatest difference, which makes all the difference, is that now I get back on my feet faster. This is how to build resilience. The more you develop your truth, the more resilient you become. You're not afraid to fall. You're not afraid to pick yourself back up. You drop the notion that it's all or nothing. You realize life has ups and downs, and it's all totally normal. You can start living a miraculous life today. It's not that the fear, judgment, and negativity won't ever creep in again, but if and when they do, you'll have the courage, strength, and love for yourself to get back up and keep living your life. Keep living your joy. Keep living your love.

This is why the Torah word for God means the eternal present and symbolizes an ever-present unfolding of the infinite light that we know as perfect compassion and love. But you don't have to be religious to know that there is a power greater than what you can perceive. Deepak Chopra often says that quantum physics isn't stranger than you think it is; it is stranger than you can think. Today much of the world understands that what we see with our eyes is truly only a fraction of the reality that exists.

Max Planck, who is considered the father of quantum physics, lived his life in a desperate pursuit of understanding the laws of the physical universe. He wanted to understand matter, the essence of a table and chair, why things fall down and not up, and how the light of the sun creates a rainbow. In his process, he accidentally, and unhappily, discovered that in truth, there is nothing physical about our universe at all. The world is an ocean of motion, vibrating energy that manifests itself as something that appears to be physical when, at its core, it is pure energy. This is a quotation from Planck's Nobel Prize acceptance speech:

As a physicist who has devoted his whole life to rational science, to the study of matter . . . I would like to say that my research on the atom has shown me that there is no such thing as matter in itself. What we perceive as matter is merely the manifestation of a force that brings the particles of an atom to vibration and holds them together in the tiniest solar system of the universe. . . . We must assume that this force that is active within the atom comes from a conscious and intelligent Mind. This Mind is the ultimate source of matter.[4]

In his discovery of this Universal Mind, Planck gave scientific language to what all spiritual paths have been discussing throughout the entirety of history. *A Course in Miracles* says that "a Universal theology is impossible. But a Universal experience is not only possible, it is necessary."[5] This is the One Universal Loving Presence that is interconnected within and above all things that we can perceive with our senses. You are in It, and It is within you. This presence is what Kaballa calls the *shechina*, which literally means "Dwelling Presence."

I use the acronym GUIDE (**G**uiding, **U**niversal & unified **I**ntelligence, and **D**ynamic **E**nergy) as a reminder that you are always being guided by a divine presence, pointing you in the direction that you want to go and helping you achieve all the aspirations you set out to accomplish.

> **G:** *Guiding.* This is a reflection of omnipotence, meaning all-powerful, a limitless capacity to take part in everything in your life. There are no accidents. Everything is purposeful and leads you to your highest good.

> **UI:** *Universal & unified Intelligence.* This is a reflection of omniscience, meaning all-knowing. There is a constant and complete awareness of the past, present, and future, a complete knowing of everything that leads to the highest good and best possible outcome. It is this consciousness that underlies everything. It is perfect divine intelligence.

DE: *Dynamic Energy.* This is a reflection of omnipresence, meaning all-present, a presence that is always everywhere at the same time. This intelligence shares information and brings life and consciousness into being. Like the electricity in a home, it is the power source that infuses and directs energy into everything that's plugged in. All of reality, including the past, present, and future, is connected to the One manifesting presence, i.e., the power source and energy of the world, the Eternal *Being* that causes all energy to come into being at every moment. This is the energy of love.

All of life is a movement of love, from love, to love. There is an entanglement, an interconnectedness between all things in this world. We are all connected—all humans, animals, plants, and the earth itself. Nothing in the world is disconnected from other things. On the surface, it may seem that way, but when we look deeper, we understand that we're all connected. Thus, everything is seen, known, and understood. Everything is shared. You are not separate from anything in the world because all of our energy is from the same source. We are animated by the same energy, and therefore we are energetically connected to everything. That is why when you think and speak positively and elevate your personal energy, everything in the world is elevated as well. We are, in fact, One.

Take this idea of having a GUIDE with you everywhere you go, knowing that you are being held by a perfect intelligence that is in everything, everywhere, always. When you tune in to the frequency of divine guidance, you are shown exactly where to go. You will know you're tuned in because it feels good and you'll be happy, at peace, and enjoying the moment.

Remember the shoe called you? Well, that's not just true for you; it's true for the whole Universe. We look at the Universe and think we know what we're looking at. We're convinced that we know how the world works and why things are happening in our lives. It is because you woke up late that you missed the bus, and it's because your coworkers conspired against you that you were fired. It's because you put in the extra twelve hours of work that you got that promotion and because you are more creative that you got the gig. When we look at life in this way, we're only ever looking at the shoe. It's superficial. There is a whole Being that fits into that shoe and is infinitely bigger than anything we can imagine. That Being is the source of life itself and is guiding everything that happens in your life. It is the love of the Universe and the energy that pervades everything, everywhere, always.

Tools and Practice

For just a moment, let's turn our attention back to the Map. In the beginning, this idea of certainty is just a thought; then it transcends and becomes a belief. But as you go deeper into yourself and sense the spirit of it, there is a knowing. This knowing allows you to accept and feel the pain as real yet not allow it to take over your life. You can begin to forgive and accept the unacceptable. There are some things you can start doing today that will allow you to access the power of inner certainty and live with more trust and faith and with a knowing that your life is in a good place.

Look for synchronicity: The more you look for grace, the more grace you'll notice. It's no accident that people who talk about experiencing miracles in their life seem to experience them all the time. That means that as the story of life unfolds, we have the opportunity to put some of the pieces together and see that, in fact, things are working out a lot more than we realize.

As an experiment, choose something you perceive as a blessing in your life and trace through all the events that needed to happen for you to attain it. You might be surprised to find that there was some darkness on the way. There is a Kabbalistic principle that the peel always precedes the fruit. This is the power of hindsight. We can look back and see that whatever happened was purposeful, as it led to another blessing in our life.

This is something you should become used to doing constantly. Just keep your eyes open to the sights and sounds of the signs. The next time something happens in your life, even something as trivial as a traffic jam or being late to work, see it as an opportunity. Somewhere in the back of your mind, be open to seeing how this event will work out and how love is hidden in it. Sometimes the fact that you didn't get frustrated and instead waited to see a loving response is, in itself, a miracle. Maybe you usually become frustrated when you're late, and this time you were relaxed and kept a smile on your face. These subtle shifts in your perspective are already miraculous and will lead to you seeing more and more synchronicity in your life.

Let me share a simple yet profound example. One morning, I woke up early and headed to the workspace where I had been studying, developing my practice, and working on writing this book. It's a pretty big commercial building that's mostly taken up by different tech companies, but a small office space is used by several of us to share group learning and develop our practices.

At the entrance is a small boutique café, and that day I decided to pick up a salad for lunch. The man at the counter said it would be 20 shekels (roughly $5), so I pulled out a 20, handed it to him, and started walking away.

"Hey, hey, not so fast, buddy. I can't take this," the man said. When I asked why not, he pointed to the bill, showing me that it had been ripped down the middle and taped back together. "I just can't have this on my head to deal with, so you're going to have to use something else." A little thrown off, I took back my bill and was forced to break a 50 instead.

OK, it's all for the best. There is good somewhere in here, I said to myself. I got my change and headed to the office.

We had been experiencing a bit of a heat wave in recent weeks, but when I walked out of the building at the end of the day, the wind had taken over, and it was freezing. I didn't have a jacket or a sweater, but I was right across the street from a clothing store

I like. So I ran across the street as fast as I could, shivering all the way. When I finally got to the store, I noticed a sign in the window that read, "All sweaters on sale for 119 [shekels]." I was thrilled and looked forward to being warm.

After looking at the selection, I found a distinctive, beautiful forest-green sweater and went to the counter to buy it. Just as it had said outside, the total was 119 shekels. I pulled out 220, paid for my sweater, and put it on before I got my change and headed for the bus home. When I got home, I immediately found that my wife, Avigial, loved it. My taste in clothing isn't what makes me special, so that meant a lot to me. A couple hours later, I checked my pockets and noticed that I had a single shekel when I should've had exactly 101.

"Oh, no! Either I must have left the hundred-shekel change at the store, or they forgot to give it to me," I said to my wife. We called the store, and they said that indeed, they had some extra money in the till, and I was welcome to come back, but they were closing in twenty minutes.

I jumped in the car and got there as quickly as I could. With a smile on his face, the cashier handed me 80 shekels and said, "Here you go. Thank you for shopping." I looked at him and reminded him that I had given him 220, and I only received a shekel back, so they owed me 100 even.

He continued to shake his head, saying there was only 80 extra in the register and that I must have been mistaken and only given him 200. I thought that maybe he was right, but I knew I had given 220. Then it hit me: "The twenty had a tear down the middle and was taped up!" He looked through the bills in his hand, and indeed, there was the twenty from that morning. He looked in a strangely puzzled way at the register, accepted that I was correct, and gave me the full change.

I felt such joy, not because I had gotten an extra 20 shekels but because I felt the love and guidance that surround us all the time. We just need to get out of the way and follow the lead. Imagine if I had complained or gotten upset earlier. Wouldn't I have felt stupid for being upset at the thing that had saved me my money? Or worse, imagine if I had fought with the guy at the café and forced him to take the ripped bill. That would've been it. I would've had no proof that I had paid the extra amount.

This may seem like a silly or trivial example, but it's just a small sample of what is happening around us all the time. The thing that gets in the way of the Universe's love is deciding that what's happening doesn't fit our version of how life should go. We miss the beauty of the magic that is happening. When we're open to it, we receive winks, hugs, and kisses that remind us we're on the right track, being taken care of and supported.

In the same way, something drew you to this book. That's not a small thing either. You're holding a book on how to more deeply connect and experience the Truth of who you are. I don't know what's going on in your life right now, but it wouldn't surprise me one bit if this was exactly what you needed to hear. Look for the divine providence that unfolds in your life. Make it your practice to notice how things seem to be leading and guiding you in a particular direction.

Remember the following three rules about your life's circumstances.

1. Everything has the same source.

2. It is ultimately good for you and the world.

3. It's on purpose with cosmic intention.

All of this is guiding you toward your higher good and presenting an opportunity for you to learn, develop, or express more of your spiritual potential. Life is the ultimate game of hide-and-seek. That is actually why the Hebrew word for Universe, *Olam*, also means "hidden." The world hides the love of God, and our job is to find it. God, the energy of the Universe, is love, is good, is personal, is involved, is fair, is purposeful, is patient, and is waiting for you. You will always receive exactly what you need for the next step in your spiritual evolution.

Open up a dialogue: There is a reason that all religions have some form of prayer worship. Something magical and powerful happens when you open your mouth and express your humanity toward the loving energy of life. Intelligence and our ability to verbally express how we think and feel are part of what makes us human. We can choose to use our words to connect or disconnect. Making time to have a personal dialogue with the Intelligence of the Universe will change your life.

This is a time to express gratitude for what is going well in our lives. We spend so much time complaining. Imagine if we used all that energy to sit in gratitude instead. You can shift the energy inside you from one of mediocrity to one of greatness. See how the world is abundant, and express it. There is a verse in Psalms that says, "It is good to thank God."[6] It's not just saying that it's a good thing to thank God; it is saying that the *definition of good* is to live in abundance, to live in appreciation of what is, to live in gratitude. That is the essential definition of good.

In addition to being thankful, use this time to ask for guidance and support in areas you could use help in. Ask for clarity, and if you choose, even ask for a sign. Be playful. This is not something to overthink. When you do engage in dialogue, don't let it end with your side of the conversation. Stay aware as the day or week unfolds and notice whether what you desire appears in your life. Life speaks to us in mysterious ways. Sometimes you'll be hit with clarity by a bumper sticker on the back of someone's car, and other times, things will be crystal clear as the love of your life walks in the door.

There are three reasons to take your desires from thought to speech. The first is that speech acts as a catalyst to open your channel and feel what you're talking about. Often you could be blocked, and just getting the words out of your mouth can help move you emotionally. The second reason is that sometimes you may think you know what you're feeling, and then when you open your mouth, you realize there was more beneath the surface. Just thinking or meditating may not be a full reflection of all the things you truly want to express. Sometimes you have to say them. The third reason is that when you speak, you are actively bringing ideas that exist in the dimension of thought into the more concrete dimension of speech. In doing so, you activate more of that power to express itself in your life. You ultimately become a channel for blessing in your life and the lives of others. This is why authenticity is much more important than the words you say. More important than what you think and say is what you feel and want.

Although it's ideal to set aside time and open a dialogue, my most powerful moments happen on the go. I definitely enjoy my morning meditation, intention setting, gratitude practice, and prayer, but there is something magical about carrying that with you when you're running around. Some of the greatest experiences I've had came from a quick and quiet conversation or a sentence I sent out to the Universe that had almost immediate results, which in turn sent me back with more gratitude, more connection, and more certainty. This is something you should not underestimate. It is a tool that can take you to the top of the world when you realize how impactful it is.

In addition to all the previously mentioned reasons for prayer, there is another very powerful one: when you pray, you let your ego take a back seat because in prayer, you acknowledge that you don't have all the answers yet. As I mentioned earlier, the main block to experiencing the Truth of certainty is the ego. The ego idea that we're in control stops our ability to receive. We want to be in a state of allowing in which we dance with life and see things unfold without the notion that we're in control. When we pray, we consciously remind ourselves that we can't solve the problems. We can only be open to receiving the answers.

Meditate: In the same vein, I can't overstate the power of meditation. Daily meditation has literally changed my life and is something I am eternally grateful for. There are so many different versions of meditation, but even something as simple as conscious breathing can be replete with benefits. If prayer is you speaking to God, meditation is clearing the space for God to speak back. There is so much noise going on outside and even more noise going on inside our heads. In stillness and silence, we can forget about the illusion and instead reconnect with the essence of who we are.

Watch, read, and listen: The more you read about and engage in discussions on the subject of certainty, the more certainty you will create, furthering your awareness of it. It's very important to keep yourself plugged in to all the different teachers, books, and audio guides that explore the ideas of certainty, faith, trust, and knowing. It is better to miss a meal than to miss a day of growing your mind and nurturing your soul.

Change your perception: Change the way you look at your role. Be a space creator. It's very likely that you still think solely in terms of cause and effect. You input certain energy, and the outcome is attached to what you put in. So if you worked hard enough, strongly enough, and quickly enough, or were pretty enough, rich enough, and so on, you would be successful, and if not, then you wouldn't be.

Unlearn this belief. Meditate on the idea that your input is not what creates the output. It creates the space for the Universe to come in and act through you. When we think we're in charge, our world can feel chaotic and out of order because it is. But when we let go and realize the outcome isn't ours to decide, regardless of how well we perform, we can step into peace. The idea that all things take place as cause and effect in a physical sense is an illusion. The outcome is part of a higher order of reality, and our job is to create the space for it to enter.

The idea of self-sacrifice and giving it your all means exactly what the words say. Give it your all but not more than your all. Sometimes we push too hard. We usurp control of the situation and decide that all of the responsibility for getting something done is ours. That approach is nothing more than fear and ego. Giving it your all means wrestling with all that you have without destroying yourself in the process. If you pushed any machinery to its maximum capacity for an extended period of time, you would break it. If you push your body, emotions, and soul too hard without nurturing them, you will break. Give it your all but not more than that. You're simply making space for it to manifest.

Unlearning this belief will also force you to lean on the Universe and rely on a loving, guiding Source energy. If you can have fun in the process, you will open up a channel to draw guidance and a flow of blessing into your life. Playing is trusting. We play when we feel safe. Sometimes you will have to let go of logic and let something deeper guide you. Listen to your intuition. It's OK to mess up. Practice failing. Practice falling. Practice taking small risks that will have big rewards for you. Life can and will do for you what you can't do for yourself. Practice letting go. Practice trust. Know with certainty that you will receive the exact help you need for your purpose.

The very first line of *The Shulchan Aruch*, the book of codified Torah wisdom, states that you should "place God in front of you always, this is the way of the righteous."[7] On the surface, what this means is that we should remain in a state of higher consciousness no matter what we are involved in, trusting and engaging in life from a place of knowing that everything is being manifested from One Loving Source. As we go through life, we must stay present and pay attention to how everything fits together.

The Baal Shem Tov elaborates that when you live in a state of equanimity, in a peaceful state of knowing that everything is a reflection of God's Love for you, outcomes will matter less to you. You won't be bothered by what someone says or does to you, what your life circumstances are, or what you've done. This is awakening. This is consciousness. This is also the end of ego: to be conscious that every happening, every thought and action of another human being, is divinely guided by an inner light of love. In this awareness, what happens on the outside makes no difference because you know it's from the same Loving Source that guides you and the world toward the highest possible good. The world is always working *for* you, not against you.

God gives wisdom to the wise. Practice thinking "good." Make it a ritual. Repetition makes mastery. If you don't feel strong enough, practice surrendering to love and asking for a better mindset by saying, "I surrender to you, God (or Source Energy/Loving Source). I am ready to receive a better mindset and perspective. I want to see the situation better. Let love and positivity enter, and allow me to see things in a new way."

"In the good days, be fully in the good. And in the bad days, see," says Ecclesiastes.[8] When things are going well, bask in the glory of gratitude, and when things seem to be going against you, keep looking. Don't let the world decide how you will experience it. You decide how you will experience the world.

The Zohar says that heroes are born from those who overcome negative thinking and see with eyes of love. When you start the process of looking for the soul of the world, the hidden messages and wisdom, you create a channel for God to send you divine insight and clarity. Go create, and you will be created. You create the space. If you choose to love life, love will fill it, and you will see the hidden good. If you want to truly live, love your days and look for the good.

When you know that on the inside of everything there is real love for you and all that is, then what is happening on the outer layer makes no difference. Focus on what is inside. This is the pathway to peace. This is the pathway to love.

In the next chapter, we'll dive into the condition of joy. The way you feel is a direct reflection of what you really believe about yourself and your life. This is the testing ground for knowing how deeply you are living in alignment with inner Truth.

CHAPTER SIX

The Condition of Joy

Joy comes from within. It is not tied to events, things or circum-
stances, like landing a new job, buying a new car or celebrating
a birthday. Joy is more like an attitude. It comes from a spiritu-
al place, no matter what your spiritual belief might be. It comes
from inner contentedness and worthiness. From feeling connect-
ed to self and others. Joy is present regardless of circumstances.
—KALEIGH MCMORDIE, MCN, RDN

Now that we've taken a look at the first two conditions, intention and certainty, we can jump into the most crucial condition of your life's journey: the condition of joy. This is really the litmus test for how deeply you're living in alignment with intention and certainty. It means your vibrational energy is back to its natural state. You feel good because you're feeling God. You feel good because you know who you are and you fearlessly enjoy your life. You feel good because you're not weighed down by the past or afraid of the future; you know things are always working out for you. You feel good because you are totally present with yourself, your friends and family, and your creative projects. You feel good because joy is your nature. This joy is unconditional.

This condition asserts that your state of consciousness is more essential than your behaviors, that inside is just as, or more, important than outside. In a truly awakened state of consciousness, your natural feeling is unconditional joy. It's an inner calm, a good and high-vibrational energy that you naturally carry. Our inner experience of joy is a measuring stick of how much we're living in the first two conditions. You can always check your emotional pulse and know whether you're living with the miracle mindset, if you're believing in the paradigm of love and goodness or living in fear and judgment.

We often think we will be happy when we have a good life, but only when you are happy will you have a good life. In *The Four Agreements*, Don Miguel Ruiz writes, "When you feel good, everything around you is good. When everything around you is great, everything makes you happy. You are loving everything around you because you are loving yourself."[1] It's you, not the circumstances, that generates your happiness. You are the one who gets to bring happiness to every circumstance you encounter. We truly don't see things as they are. We see them as *we* are.

Your joy is not only a measurement of how well you are leaning into your truth but also a channel opener for you to go even more deeply into that space, which means it becomes difficult to do anything meaningful and creative when you are feeling out of alignment. When I am feeling low, it can be challenging for me to move anything or anyone. You can't see how everything is working for you when you are in a low space. When you are negative, angry, complaining, or afraid, you can't see things with certainty, and it becomes hard to live with intention.

It may be obvious, but when you are feeling good, life is more fun and enjoyable, everything you do is better, and people want to be around you. Why? Because when you are happy and positive, you see the good in what's going on. You notice the good in others. And when you're focusing on what's going well and what is good, you behave differently. You are more subtle with criticism when it's needed and don't react as strongly when you receive it. You don't have strong reactions when things "go wrong" or when people make comments that would normally hurt. You find it much easier to look the other way and be pleasant in your life.

In the book *You Can Be Happy No Matter What*, Dr. Richard Carlson writes, "When we feel better, we have more access to our own wisdom and common sense. We tend to be less reactive, defensive, and critical; we make better decisions and we communicate more effectively." He goes on to say that "a contented feeling brings with it a childlike enjoyment—a lighthearted way of being in the world that opens a channel of appreciation for simple things, to feel grateful for the magnificent gift of life itself."[2] He then describes this contented state of mind as a state of love. Love, my friend. That's what this story is all about. When you are living with love, you shine love on everyone you meet. You beam love into every place you go and infuse all you do with your spirit. When you live with the light of the world, you become a light in the world.

There is a verse that says that even if one were to keep all of the rules written in the Torah, if one is not happy and living in gratitude in the process, one will be sent into exile. This punishment seems harsh, but the metaphor is that even if you live a devoted life full of spiritual rituals, if you aren't experiencing the joy of life in the process, you're missing the central point of what you're doing. You're not experiencing the love of the Universe when you're living in resentment, frustration, or apathy. Exile is a symbol of being sent out of your natural state. To live in exile is to live in a foreign place that is not your own. When you aren't in joy, you aren't yourself. The path to your personal salvation reveals itself when you plug back in to your happiness. A second verse says, "It's with joy that they left [exile]."[3] Being joyful is the pathway back to you because joy is your nature. The positive experience of being joyful directly impacts and elevates your decision-making, behaviors, relationships, bodily health, creativity, inner knowing, and intuition, and the Zohar says it literally changes the providence in your life. It is this energy of joy that extends the BRANCHes of the miracle mindset. Being happy isn't just important; it is intelligent!

We understate the power of happiness. If we could feel truly happy and alive, we would perform at a totally different level all the time. When we are in a high state, we perform better and live better. That creates better actions and better results, which increases our belief in ourselves and our power to create. And here is the fun part: life stops being about the performance because you're already right where you want to be. A better life is a by-product of being right where you are. One of the most important decisions you can make is to turn to joy as often as possible. Yes, happiness is a choice: the choice of intention, which is to be who you truly are, and the choice of certainty, which is to see the world how it truly is. You will learn how to make and keep the commitment to feeling good. It is a gift that keeps giving.

Your joy is both a barometer for how well you're living and a gateway for living in alignment and knowing your truth. I like to ask groups I speak to if happiness is a luxury or a necessity. A luxury is something you would want to have if you could. A necessity is something that you need to have. What if I framed the question this way: Is your soul a luxury or a necessity? Well, your soul is not something that you get. It's not something that you *have*. It's something that you *are*. This is one of the key ideas to living a truly successful and fulfilling life, living a joyous life. When you feel who you are, you feel joy. Being more means feeling more joy.

So here is the big question: Why aren't we all naturally joyful all the time? Why can life often seem more daunting and stressful than joyful and light? Here is the short story of our lives: we want the things we want because what we really want is to *feel* a certain way. We all want to feel safe, secure, and taken care of. We want to feel love, joy, and connection. We want to feel valuable, worthy, and good. We want to feel authentic, genuine, and kind. What we all really want is to feel complete and whole. We want to experience fulfillment. Nevertheless, as I mentioned earlier, because of our upbringing and physical nature, we experience a deep sense of lack. We feel that we have to do something, get somewhere, or have some pleasurable experience in order to feel this love and fulfillment. I've called this the *if-there-then* distortion. We believe we'll be happy only *if* a set of conditions are met, when we get *there* in space and *then* in time.

We've gotten lost in the illusion of the world and haven't been able to get out. Here and there, we get a glimpse and a taste of it, but in essence we are attracted to the beauty and promise of pleasure, be it physical or emotional. We want to feel good and be good, but we've lost our internal compass that directs us to where to find what we're really looking for. Then, when we don't get that good feeling, we end up not feeling good enough, experiencing feelings such as shame, inauthenticity, sadness, anger, frustration, depression, loneliness, weakness, fear, lack, and emptiness. This only further increases our desire to feel good. So then we keep trying to fill this void and desire with physical things, social status and power, relationships, pleasure, and experiences. Inevitably, we either fail and fall, bringing us back to square one, or we achieve and grieve the fact that we still feel a lack of fulfillment. Success without fulfillment is the ultimate failure. People don't really buy things; people buy feelings. People buy states of consciousness. We all want to feel that good feeling we call fulfillment.

We're all together in this search for wholeness, but we've gotten the wrong message about where to find it. This is what the Torah calls *Yetzer Hara*, or the undeveloped perspective to search for love in all the wrong places. This distorted view of reality tells us we will be happy *if-there-then*. "If I get that thing, when I get to the place over there, or when it's that time in the future, then and only then will I feel happy." As long as we believe this lie, we will continue to run around in circles for a really long time.

So how do we find joy? Where is it, really? How do we live with more joy today? When you cut out everything that's not you, you will feel joy. Remember, you are good, perfect, and safe, and you have an innate desire to love creatively. That is the Truth of who you are. You are constantly being guided and directed to realize this Truth. You become good not by trying to be good but by finding the goodness that is already within you and allowing it to emerge. But it can emerge only if something in your state of consciousness fundamentally changes. It's all about waking up. It's all about remembering.

When you start reinterpreting who you are, what you are doing here, and how the world works, you will start moving closer and closer to the Truth that the real you is already good and perfect. The Universe is a loving place, and you have a powerful role to play in it. You are not born with nothing; you are born with everything. The world is loud, and the soul is soft. Truth speaks in a whisper.

The Four Spirit Principles of Joy

Spirit Principle #1: No-thing can make you happy!

Joy is your birthright and the channel of your spirit. As with a radio, when you tune in to this station, you experience your nature. If nothing were wrong in your life, you would be happy. If you didn't judge what you should or shouldn't be doing, if you didn't judge what others are doing or what life presents to you, you would feel good. When you stop running to the future and holding on to the past, you'll feel good. There is only ever joy in the present. Be here and be joyful here.

We often think that when we get more things done and accomplish bigger feats, we'll feel better about ourselves. The truth is when you do less, you feel joy more. I'm not saying that doing more is bad; I'm saying the compulsive need to do more is the wrong mindset. You don't ever have to do "more"; you have to do "good." It's the spiritual quality of what you do that truly matters.

In Ecclesiastes, King Solomon says, "Everything is vanity,"[4] meaning every "thing" is empty on its own. No thing, no title, nothing that you garner on this physical plane will give you the joy and fulfillment that you are truly looking for. Only finding your true Self will bring you joy. We have to collectively change our definition of success from accomplishment and achievement to alignment, being in a state of joy, and loving our life as we journey toward our goals and desires.

Spirit Principle #2: You don't have to search for happiness. You just need to see the barriers to it and remove them.

After I tell people that nothing can make them happy, the response I usually get is "Well, then, what will make me happy? How do I get it?" The problem is the question. The question implies that you have to go out and get happiness. But remember, joy isn't something you find; it's something you reveal because it's something that you are. When you stop living in everything that you're not, the result is joy. Life, liberty, and the pursuit of happiness. Interestingly, the pursuit of happiness is what keeps you from your natural wellspring of joy. It doesn't mean you can't have pursuits, goals, and desires—no, not at all. But instead of *pursuing* happiness, pursue what you love from a place *of* happiness, which is your inner light.

When Michelangelo was asked how he had made a beautiful sculpture of a horse, he said, "I didn't. I just cut away everything that wasn't a horse." Similarly, you can find your natural state by cutting away everything that isn't you. You don't need to find happiness. The search is over. All you have to do is go up to the wall that has been keeping it out and start taking it down. What is the wall? What is the barrier?

Spirit Principle #3: When we trade our faith for fear, we trade our joy for pain.

What's keeping us unhappy? What is blocking us from our joy? We will now come full circle: what blocks us is fear. At a certain point in our life, we started fearing more than loving. That was an important part of our development because there is healthy as well as unhealthy fear. It's important to know that when there is an armed robber, you should run and protect yourself. Fear is important to keep us from falling off the edge of a cliff or running a red light. But the human mind has distorted the essence of fear and turned it into the background soundtrack of our lives without our even realizing it.

In the condition of intention, we spoke about the fear of not living fully as your Self. In the condition of certainty, we spoke about the need to be in control, fearing the outcomes of your life's experiences. Fear, my friend, is what influences you to make decisions that deny the Truth of who you really are, leading you to experience the pain of not being the true you. We feel pain when we're not being ourselves. We feel pain when we think we're in control. We feel pain when we fall out of alignment with Truth.

There's a proverb that says, "It's better to be a living dog than a dead lion," meaning it is better to be a living version of yourself (even if it's a dog) than a dried-up, dead version of someone or something that you're not (even if it's seemingly the king of the jungle). If it's not really you, then it's not real.

Spirit Principle #4: When you restore your faith in love, you will return to joy.

The root of all our fears is that we've fallen out of love with life. Life is a magical dance when we are in love. We fall out of love when we lose the conditions of intention and certainty and forget who we are and what life is all about. When we lose ourselves and our connection to the Infinite Source of light, love, and perfection, we feel fearful, weak, and alone. This is spiritual unconsciousness. Remember that your inner being never leaves you. You are always being held. You don't have to live in fear of what other people think, and you don't need to have anything to feel worthy. The truth is you have to be true to yourself, true to your soul, and true to the source of all good. You are meant to be happy. You are meant to enjoy your life.

The question then becomes, what happens if I don't believe in myself anymore? What if I don't believe in the love of the Universe? What happens when I am feeling down and out and can't seem to get myself thinking the right way? In the darkness, we can lose sight of why we're here. We can lose sight of our purpose, our connection to the Universe, and any kind of Godly experience. Even if we understand it intellectually, it still doesn't help when we feel the pain and hurt. When we feel disconnected, everything just looks dark. This is when we need to use joy as a channel to bring us back into ourselves. We need joy to bring us back to our intention for living and the certainty of love. What can we do when we are in a low energy space?

Over time, I realized that when we're in a low space, we are totally focused on what we *don't* want instead of what we *do* want. We mentally emphasize the problem and are less likely to pay attention to what we'd like instead. As I mentioned in the condition of intention, you become powerful when you know what you want and are solution-focused rather than focused on what's going wrong and what you don't want.

The question to start asking yourself is what can I do right now to feel more joy? What can I do to get some relief from the pain? What thoughts do I need to think, whom do I need to be with, where do I need to go, and what actions do I need to take? Sometimes it is as simple as a little reminder that you keep on your wall. You can make an inspiration or motivation board to look at when you lose your feeling of connection. Just reading a few sentences about your purpose and power can awaken you to everything you want to be.

Maybe you avoid calling a certain friend when you're feeling low, but deep down, you know that when you're on the phone with them, they pick you up. Make it a habit to call them when you feel low. This habit is the best gift you can give yourself. It can save you hours, if not days, of waiting around in a slump. There are things you can do right now to get back into your great inner state. Sometimes you just have to do something fun and change the way you're acting. Dance, exercise, sing, play, and have fun. If you can get yourself up and go for it, you'll be grateful afterward.

When we fall out of sync, we lose touch with our power, so get yourself laughing. Whether it's from watching a funny clip, writing about some hilarious times you've had with friends, or doing something silly, when you're laughing, your body is remembering that laughter is natural, and that is where you want to be. You can even fake it if you need to. Laugh out loud for sixty seconds and see how you feel when you're done. You won't regret it.

If you really want to pick up your mood and feel good, go out and do good by performing an act of kindness. Call your parents or grandparents and thank them for anything you are grateful for. Let them know you care. Go into a store and smile at someone. Do you know how happy you make people when you smile at them? They feel noticed, they feel that you are happy with them, and they feel your energy. I challenge you to make eye contact and smile at ten random people when you go out. You will feel better, guaranteed! If you can afford to, go to a coffee shop and buy someone's coffee. Be creative with how you can be and do good in the world. You will certainly feel better when you're finished.

While I was working on this book, I was supercharged and excited about it every day. I was writing and sharing and really leaning into the principles I've shared with you so far, and as a result, I was experiencing miracle after miracle in my life. I started recording meditative sparks of inspiration and sending them out to my email list on the weekends. The response was magnetic. People were really loving what I was doing, and I knew it had more to do with my energy than with the words I was saying.

One week, I seriously overworked myself and ironically felt a little too in control of what I was doing. I was completely depleted of energy, and next thing I knew, it was Friday morning, and I had to get to my computer to make the next audio class. I turned the computer on, loaded the program, and set up my recording gear. The whole time, I felt that I *had* to do it, even though I was tired, depleted, and uninspired. I was about to click "record" when I thought, *I am not trusting right now.* I took a moment to say a silent blessing, asking for guidance and clarity, and then I stopped. I didn't record a thing.

I turned off the programs and the computer, put away my equipment, and went out to the forest to meditate, write in my journal, and reconnect to Spirit. I ended up taking that whole weekend off to rearrange my energy. On Monday morning, I woke up and felt fully energized and plugged in. I was given deep insight that day and had several breakthroughs in my work and relationships. The best part of the weekend, though, was the reminder that the most important thing I could do for myself was committing to feeling good and sticking to my spiritual practice. This is what will move you from feeling mediocre to feeling amazing and living the miraculous life you were meant to live.

It's all about being present. Nothing will give you more access to joy than being totally in the now. It's our dramas about the past and our worries about the future that keep us from our most powerful possession. If you can't be here and now, then you can't be there and then, because when there and then becomes right now, you'll be there and then again. Later is a lie. I once walked into a bar with a sign in front that said, "Free beer tomorrow." I thought that was so funny. The promise of the future is tempting, but you have to know that today is all there ever is because "tomorrow" never comes.

Here are a few tips to keep in mind as you expand your spiritual practice and ground yourself in the present moment.

Listen to your body: Even though sometimes it's the body that gets us into trouble, more often than not, your body knows when something is bad for it. Don't do anything that ends in physical pain or lack of consciousness. Overindulging in any physical pleasure ultimately leads to pain. Don't confuse pleasure with joy. Don't confuse a high with true happiness. Although metaphorically, you are the rider and the body is the horse, you can't get anywhere if the horse isn't feeling well.

Getting yourself to exercise can be hard, yet you know that when you're finished with your routine, you'll feel amazing and pumped for life. Listen to your body. It wants healthy food, it wants exercise, and it wants enough sleep. Your body is the instrument you have been given while you are here. When you learn how to play it, its song is beautiful.

Listen to your loving community: We all have the ability to create and find a loving community, whether it's our family, friends, and coworkers or a group we're a part of. These are the people in our lives who truly care and want the best for us. Often we get lost in ideas we think are good, but it is really important to share what we are excited about or working on with others. They may have great and often surprising insight into what you are doing. Embrace what you have in the people you are surrounded by.

Live by a code: Don't throw away the foundations that were discovered and passed down by your ancestors. Pain, struggle, and thousands of years of life experience went into creating what was created. It is a gift to have a code to rely on. Even though you haven't reached all of the spiritual plateaus they passed through, you can live a more conscious life, even when you're not fully conscious. That is such a blessing. Living by a spiritual code will help you live a truly joyful life. Sure, you can learn from your mistakes, but you can learn from others' mistakes as well.

A good example of a code that works is the twelve-step program. Since it was designed for people who struggle painfully with addiction, it had to be a powerful and clear code that would allow a person to live a joyous, successful life without the debilitating addiction. There are many who just want to "be happy" using and doing whatever they are addicted to. Thank God there are people who experienced it first and led the way toward miraculous recovery.

I choose to live by the code of the Torah. For me, this is what grounds me in a reality greater than my own. My spiritual practice gives me energy and reminds me of who I really am and what I am doing here. It is what led me to writing this book. I have committed to following my inner guide and doing what's good for me, even when I don't "feel" like it. I'll be the first to tell you it is totally possible to be religious and not spiritual. You can be religious and not healthy, religious and not happy, religious and not really yourself. If that is what religion is doing to you, then you're doing it wrong. Its primary function is spiritual awakening. If it puts you to sleep, you're missing something.

Schools, businesses, and social events all have a code of conduct, even if they aren't formally written down. Living amicably in society isn't a religious duty; it is a service we collectively provide for one another. We naturally reject the concept of having rules, but everything in life is made up of rules. There are rules in nature, in sports, and in commerce. Rules are what create a space for us to live in. Nevertheless, man-made code is subject to error, and therefore the most important questions to keep in mind are the following: Is this bringing me closer to love? Is this part of my soul's agenda? Is this bringing me closer to consciousness, or is it dragging me down into a deeper spiritual sleep? Is this harmful to me or others? However you want to phrase it, it is crucial to have a sincere inner awareness of what you are doing.

Listen to your soul: Intuitively, we can all feel when we're around people who aren't good for us. There is an inner knowing that *I probably shouldn't do this or go there.* Listen to yourself. You're not making it up. Sometimes the flip side is true: you get a feeling that you have to go somewhere or do something. Listen to what's going on inside you, even if it's out of the ordinary. It takes a bit of practice and sensitivity to sense the difference between an immature desire and an intuitive calling, so check in with your body, your community, and the code you live by. Are these things bringing you closer to or further from your Self?

There is a deep power in silence and meditation that brings you to a place beyond the senses. It takes you beyond your belief about life and into the space of life itself. Take a break from trying to *become* and just *be.* That means doing the things that make you happy and practicing being present and fully in the here-now. Listen to the inner urge to spend more time serving others. Find ways to experience love and kindness as often as possible, and you will automatically start to experience the true nature of your soul. You don't need to start an organization or donate a large sum of money to a charity. You could simply schedule some time to call your grandmother or smile and say good morning to someone walking down the street. Being of service is the mindset of being a contributing member of society and the world around you. It's about getting outside yourself and becoming sensitive to the needs of others. For example, instead of thinking about what I want to say to my friend who just went through a breakup, I can consider what they need to hear in that moment, or I could say nothing at all and just be present for them.

Don't Be Apologetic about How You Want to Feel

Most of all, don't be apologetic about how you want to feel. Of course you want to feel good. You always want to feel good. That's how we were created. That is such an important part of your spiritual practice. It indicates how much you are leaning into Truth, into your reason for being. It doesn't mean you will always be happy. Far from it. But what it does mean is that you can transform your life from periodically experiencing happy moments to feeling a general sense of peace and joy in your day-to-day life. This will immediately change the way you experience life and respond to its situations through your general behavior.

I remember when I had my first breakthrough awakening experience, and it was so energetic that I didn't know what to do with myself. I hadn't changed anything in my life just yet, but I was a new person. Everyone I ran into kept telling me that I seemed lighter, had so much energy, and was electric. It was such a good and positive experience. People wanted to be around me, and some even openly admitted that one of the reasons they hadn't spent time with me before was because of my heavy and overly serious attitude toward life. My productivity went through the roof. My ambition skyrocketed. I felt so comfortable in my skin and excited about life that I wanted to scream it from the rooftops. Entering this state is magical. The synchronicity and miracles I experienced on a daily basis were mind-blowing. The people I met or ran into and the things that showed up in my inbox were exactly what I needed. I was incredibly in touch with how I was feeling throughout the day and was just as interested in what was going on inside me as in what was happening around me.

Get used to gauging how you are feeling with the knowing that this is your measuring stick of how aligned you are right now. Make a habit of touching base with your emotional reality and redirecting yourself to higher and more powerful energy. Empower the conditions of intention and certainty and enjoy the life you are living.

How you feel isn't a side thing. It is a *Hey, I am right in front of you* thing. The more you learn to listen to how you're feeling, the more you can lean into the light of who you are and what you are supposed to be doing or not doing in your life. Feeling lousy is your wake-up call to remember that you're probably judging right now. Feeling good is a reminder that you are doing great and have the opportunity to feel gratitude for how you are doing. It's good to feel good. Don't let anybody take that away from you.

Sometimes when you're feeling good, you may feel some shame or guilt and think, *Everyone around me is feeling blah, but I'm feeling on top of the world.* It can be a weird place to be. Do it anyway. Joy is your birthright. If you're happy, you're helping. That's it. If you're happy, you'll make others happy. If you're in joy, you'll assist others in their joy. That is one of the greatest contributions you can make. When you are present, you can awaken the presence in others, embrace life for all that it is, and enjoy the process while watching it all unfold.

With this, I say, congratulations! We've arrived at the end of the third condition. We now know that with direct intention and certainty, your life can be one of love and purpose, and living in joy is your biofeedback system that lets you know that you are plugged in to your highest beliefs. I am excited about the next part, where we will return to the power of our thinking and speech, but this time from a whole new dimension. When you're plugged in to love and feeling good, you'll be surprised at how quickly things start to shift and manifest in your life. Let's get ready for miracles.

the Transformation *of the* Three Conditions

CHAPTER SEVEN

Synchronicity, Miracles, and Manifesting

I f they haven't already, some incredible synchronicities and miracles are about to start showing up in your life. When you are living life with intention and certainty, feeling the joy of being, and living true to your authentic self while knowing you are being supported in the process, your energy radiates positivity and starts a cosmic chain of events. Living with the miracle mindset—the BRANCHes of the Tree of Life—will open up opportunities for you to see the blessings and improvements in your behaviors, relationships, power of attraction, creativity, inspiration, insight, and healing.

In this chapter, we will first discuss the seemingly everyday, random events of synchronicity, which are actually not so random. They are the kisses, hugs, and winks from the Infinite letting you know that you are living in alignment with reality. We will also look at events that seem miraculous, including the fundamental miracle of how you react and experience life, and in the end we will investigate your unique role in co-creating your reality. When you clearly direct your intention, you have the power to manifest and partner with the Universe.

Synchronicity is a divine mode of communication. The Universe speaks to you through seemingly common happenings that occur in a way that appears to be coincidental. Have you ever been thinking about a particular band from your childhood, and the next thing you knew you heard them on the radio or in a store you just entered? It almost feels as if someone or something were listening to you. If we believe only in a reality that is causal in nature, we'd have to assume that one event had nothing to do with the other. However, from a spiritual perspective, honoring the reality that there is an energetic and causal relationship between all things, even though on the surface it appears to be a chance encounter, awakens our sense of the divine. The more we pay attention to these synchronicities, the more we start to experience them in our lives. The more you look for grace, the more grace will show up for you to see.

Miracles are an even clearer expression of divine communication. As I previously mentioned, miracles are when things are not just coincidental but are clearly for our benefit or fulfill our desires. They literally feel as if they are supernatural. From our vantage point, the more random or rare an event is, the greater the miracle. If it took five separate seemingly coincidental occurrences to line up the cards for you to achieve or experience your desired outcome, that's a greater miracle from our perspective, though in reality there is no order of difficulty when it comes to miracles from God's perspective. The Infinite is infinite, and so is the blessing.

Manifesting refers to our part in the co-creative process. Not only does this point to inspiring synchronicities and miracles that take place in your life, but successfully manifesting blessings means you are clear and direct in your communication with the divine. You play an active role in the process of miracle working.

The Three Cs of Co-creation

In chapter 1, we discussed the power of your thoughts and the messages you send out to the Universe. To catalyze the power of thoughts, we can focus on the three Cs of co-creation: consciousness, connection, and clear cooperation. The first is your state of consciousness. Being in a state of joy and being totally in the present moment are key. The second is your knowing or belief in the Infinite and the infinite possibilities of creation. Your belief in yourself and a supportive Universe is a crucial step to creation. You are always connected to Infinite potential. The third aspect is your conscious thought, speech, and action, or, in other words, the messages you send out. When you fill your thoughts and speech with positivity and faith in the Infinite, you become a powerful conduit for receiving all the blessings in the world. In other words, when you feel good, you feel connected, you are clearly focused on what you want, and you are ready to step in the direction of your desire. Let's look at these Cs one by one.

Consciousness: Awakened consciousness feels good, and one of the most important things you can do in your life is have fun and enjoy the process. The more we are awakened and living a conscious life, the more natural it is to bring fun to our day-to-day experiences. When you live with intention, there isn't an underlying pressure to prove your worthiness, and, with certainty, you can let go of your fear of the future. Being able to have fun is a sure sign you're living life the right way. This is why it feels good to learn something new. It's fun to surf once you're riding the wave, but a good teacher will assist you in enjoying the falls and wipeouts while you figure out your new skill. Life is no different.

When I say *fun*, I mean that you are excited and positive about what you're doing in life. You enjoy it, and you smile and laugh often. Life isn't heavy, overly serious, daunting, or stressful. Rather, it is light and joyous and comes with unexplainable giggles. There is an old notion that if you are having fun, you are disconnected from your purpose in life. This is simply not true.

Life can be meaningful and passionate without the heavy tension that leads to stress and perfectionism. Life has purpose and meaning, and, yes, that also means it ultimately won't feel good to overindulge in physical pleasures, addictive substances, or other activities that waste your time. But by no means is fun bad. Fun is a supercharger to everything you want in your life. It's a direct line to the love of the world. Now is the time to change the narrative you've been living with and start increasing your playfulness with life.

You see, we can talk about this now because the two main reasons we hold ourselves back from being more playful are that our intention is off or we have forgotten the world of love and the certainty that comes with it. When we are afraid of what other people will think or what will happen to our productivity, we tend to be overly cautious and step away from what makes us happy. But here is the catch: what makes us happy plugs us in to our most productive, creative selves. So sometimes you have to stop what you are doing, return to your Self, be present, and enjoy. Relax and know that if you are lighter and at peace, enjoying yourself and your life, you are doing yourself, as well as everyone else around you, a tremendous service.

There are, in fact, two types of *fun*: intentional fun and unintentional fun. Intentional fun is when you consciously stop holding an inner resistance and turn toward something you enjoy instead. Unintentional fun is when you have practiced leaning into the love of the Universe so much that life just becomes a fun place to be. It doesn't mean it's always roses and butterflies, but it means your default position is one of curiosity and excitement about the mystery of each day. When you start living life this way, your energy will be higher, and you'll become a magnet for positive outcomes.

Connection: Connection means sensing the infinite love and guidance of life. It is sensing how all things, events, and people are interrelated and connected and believing in this innate linking. Of course when you are living in certainty, you are a happier, peaceful person, and you have a rich inner world. But the fascinating part is that you don't just feel good; you also draw more good into your life. Throughout the book of Psalms, King David makes it clear that when you place your trust in the infinite power of love, you become a channel for blessing: "The one who trusts in The Source of Love will be surrounded by kindness."[1] In fact, the Zohar, the ancient Kabbalistic text, says that it is in direct proportion to your joy and connection that you will experience clear blessings in your life.

With the condition of certainty, you feel connected to the same flow that animates your life and the rest of the world. That means you're connected to the Infinite Intelligence and thus to infinite possibilities. This is such a life-empowering idea that the Talmud quotes a sage as saying that the first question you're asked after you die is whether you did business with faith. The sage isn't simply saying, "Did you have faith when you did business?" No, he is saying, "Did you turn your faith into your business?" This teaches that the most important question you can ask yourself is *Are you making it your business to grow your sense of connection, your sense of certainty?* Are you living your inner knowing like it's a full-time job? Working to expand your consciousness like it's your day job is the foundation for living your greatest life.

When your thinking is charged with the energy of belief, your inner vibration changes and sends the message out to the Master of the Universe. This is how prayer works. Your thinking has to have all three parts: clear thoughts, positive emotions, and this connection we often call faith. This three-part combination is what sends out the most powerful messages to the source of infinite potential. This faith removes all limitations and elevates your vibration so you can attract vibrations that are in harmony with your own.

Infinite potential and love are flowing everywhere, all the time. The question is, how will they be directed and manifested? The more aligned you are with the source of flow, the more you become a creative force in how they manifest and show up in your life and the lives of others. This is the deeper meaning behind the statement "If you change the way you look at things, the things you look at change." Two things happen. You become a highly energetically charged spiritual antenna that both receives and sends messages at a higher frequency. As a receiver, this means things in your life will start happening in ways that begin to seem miraculous because you are living at the frequency of miracles. When you feel happy, positive, and loving and you live in an abundant, trusting state, the Universe will surround you with all of these things. You will attract loving experiences, and abundance will enter your life.

Synchronistic and miraculous things will happen everywhere you go, with the people you meet, and in the things you do.

It's unbelievable and totally life-transforming. It's like singing the song of love all day long, dancing the most wonderful dance, and holding hands with the source of goodness at all times. The divine providence in your life changes when you enter this higher state of consciousness. People around you will notice that you seem to be living a charmed life, living totally in grace.

It isn't just an emotional scapegoat to help you feel better about yourself. It's a choice that becomes a creative act when you lean into it. When you lean into love, love leans into you. When you believe in blessings, blessings follow you wherever you go. When you expect miracles, they will present themselves. The Zohar says that joy is the frequency God is found on. When you feel happy and loving, you become a channel for good things and miracles in your life.

I once experienced incredible synchronicity that, as far as I'm concerned, was nothing less than miraculous. My wife and I were flying to Los Angeles to host a three-day seminar. As we were waiting in line to check in for our flight, my friend Sam's mother called and asked if we would look into a rehab facility in LA for Sam, as he had been at a low point in his life. Of course we said we would, but by the time we got to LA, she had sent an email saying not to worry about it because she was sure he wouldn't go, even if it was a good place. My wife suggested that Sam's mother call her brother Nick, who had had his fair share of hard times. She said she'd think about it, and that was that. The seminar went well, and I had several very moving experiences that impacted my life.

One evening not long afterward, Nick went out to a fancy restaurant with a couple of his close friends to relax and process everything that was going on in his life, and across the room, a verbal fight escalated between what seemed to be a couple having dinner. The man ranted and yelled, then jumped out of his chair and picked up a knife. After the woman successfully convinced him to put the knife down, the man stormed out of the restaurant, and Nick ran over to see if she was OK. "I'm fine, I'm fine," she said. They spoke for a couple minutes as he tried to see if there was anything he could do, but to no avail. She just wanted peace and quiet, and that was totally all right.

The next morning, Nick got a phone call from a number he didn't recognize. It was Sam's mom.

"Hi, I am looking for Nick. I got your number from Avigial and Moshe."

Nick was more than happy to take the call, but not long into the conversation, he thought he recognized her voice.

"Sorry, but were you at this restaurant last night?"

She responded, "Yes, I was. Why?"

"Well, I was the guy who came over to you after he put the knife down."

She was shocked. How could it be? What an intense synchronicity.

"That was Sam," she said. "That's why I am calling. He needs help."

Let's take a pause. *What?* That is an unbelievable coincidence. This is synchronicity at its best. No two events are random. If you try to find causation here, you won't, because it's beneath the surface. The spiritual reality and divine guidance hide in plain view. When I first heard what had happened, I was dumbfounded by that perfection of life.

The day after they spoke, I had plans to meet Sam for lunch, and I got a call from Nick asking if I could drop by his home in hopes that he could have a positive influence. I had to explain that I didn't have time, as I was speaking at an event later that evening and needed to prepare my talk. He insisted, and following the flow of the Universe, I decided to make time.

We all met on a nice afternoon, and by the time I finally left, I didn't have the time or head space to plan my speech. I was a bit flustered and a drop frustrated, and I realized I had to rearrange my thinking.

"Fine, I will just have to rely on You," I said out loud, laughing and winking at the sky. I let go and let myself be guided. The evening was beautiful, with a wonderful dinner party set in the middle of Jerusalem. About an hour into the event, I was asked to speak. I took a deep breath, said a quick prayer, and began to deliver what, in the end, was a beautiful speech about the power of connection. I felt so free. In the past, I would have stressed about the how, the what, and the when of my talk, but that day, it flowed so naturally. All the words and ideas came together in a marvelous way, and I was grateful for being in the flow. I was in the zone, and I could feel the room elevate from the talk. I needed to be in that state of flow and surrender to share that particular lesson, and I wouldn't have been in that state had I not had my afternoon delay.

When I was finished, I sat down next to a gentleman I hadn't met before.

"Rick Tucker," the man said as he stuck out his hand.

We spoke for nearly an hour. He told me how much he appreciated my speech, and then we were off discussing life. I told him all about how I used to be a performing musician and about my spiritual journey.

He looked at me with interest and asked, "Well, Moshe, what would you do today if tomorrow you got the call to go back out on tour?"

This was far from the first time I had been asked this question, yet it felt different.

"You know, Rick, for the last ten years, I would have easily told you that I am content where I am, and I wouldn't consider it. Today, though, I have grown and am open to all Universal possibilities and would have to at least think about it." We laughed together, and not long afterward, my wife and I went home.

The next morning, I woke up and did my regular daily meditation practice, and when I was finished, I set my intentions out loud: "I am ready. Whatever You want to send my way, I am open to the infinite possibilities of creativity, insight, and income. Thank you." Before I left for the office, I checked my email, and to my great surprise there was a message from one of my closest friends that read, "Hey, Moshe. Here's a new idea: come to London for three days and perform with me on three different university campuses. Flights and expenses paid plus a significant sum per gig. Would that be worth it for you?" Whoa! I stopped in my tracks. I could not believe my eyes. Had I really just been asked to go on tour the day after that conversation with Rick?

Let's jump back to the beginning of this story for just a minute. Sam's mother called my wife and me at the airport, which is seemingly a very everyday occurrence. But notice the chain of events that took place afterward, from Nick's evening at the restaurant to my being late to the event and sharing in such a way that Rick and I would have a conversation and I would be asked to go on tour the next day. This entire series of events could just as easily have been overlooked and seen as luck at best. The truth is, though, it's not that some people are lucky; it's that some people are looking.

Sometimes it sounds too good to be true. But the more I live life, the more I realize that very often, until it's that good, we are not yet fully living in the truth of what could be. That said, there is a catch, and it's where a lot of people get tripped up: you can't fake your feelings. You can't fake your inner state. You can't say, "I believe, and I choose love," and still feel low energy, resentment, and resistance to your life. If it's not real fire, it can't cook anything.

It is far more useful for you to be honest and authentic about what you do in fact believe and feel. I could not have gotten where I am today without a great therapist along the way. There was a lot of baggage to unpack, feelings to experience, and truth to uncover before I could realize the experience of ideas I knew were true. Truth is a doorway to peace. If you can say, "I don't believe this is good, and I am frustrated," then you can also say, "But I really *want* to see this as good, and I *want* to be at peace with my life situation." That's a true statement. The real Truth will always set you free.

From acknowledging where you are truthfully standing, you have the opportunity to rearrange the way you're thinking, reset your intentions, and pray for a new mindset. Acknowledge if your thinking, as it currently stands, is still out of alignment with a loving perspective of reality. Forgive yourself for thinking this way because it is the best mind you have. Your life's history is what brought you to this moment, and that was also part of the grand plan.

When I speak of forgiveness, I see it as the ability to fully accept what appears unacceptable by understanding that things couldn't be any different. It is to look beyond the behavior and see the light of the person within. It is to notice the unconscious behavior for what it is and maintain your own consciousness by not reacting to what's happening on the outer layer. So forgive yourself for having negative and judgmental thoughts because those thoughts are not your true Self. Let them go. Release them. And set your intentions or pray for a new way to look at things.

We are hardwired to make the best decisions possible. Nobody purposely makes a bad decision (unless in that moment they actually thought it was a good decision to make a bad decision). That's just how we're programmed. Whenever anybody does anything, has a thought, says some words, or acts in a certain way, the fascinating and sometimes hard reality is knowing they really couldn't have done better. That was actually the best they could have done in the moment, but had they been more conscious or more aware or had more access to their deeper knowing, they would have done things differently. This is the true opening for forgiveness. Forgiveness is seeing someone for who they truly are and not how they acted. It means coming to a simple acceptance that we are, in fact, human, and, as humans, we have times when we are in alignment and times when we're not. As Ecclesiastes says, "There is no righteous individual on earth that does good and yet doesn't make mistakes."[2] People don't reach for bad decisions. Neale Donald Walsch says it best: "Understanding replaces forgiveness in the mind of the master."[3] Understanding that our best mind brought us here replaces the need for forgiveness because we realize what's really happening.

One of the easiest ways to bring yourself back into a faith state is to remember that even your mistakes are there to teach you something and guide you somewhere. You can harness the power of gratitude to bring you back. One verse in Psalms says, "This is the gateway to God, the righteous enter it."[4] But it doesn't say how to get into the gateway. It just says that it exists. However, a second verse says, "Enter His gates with gratitude."[5] This is the easiest way into the gateway of the loving presence of life. Be grateful for what is, and you will find yourself living on the most powerful frequency that exists.

You don't have to know how it's going to happen. You don't have to know how you're going to get there. You simply don't, and often can't, see the way you're going to get out of where you are, but all you have to do is believe and know that it's possible, and a power greater than you will come and fill the space that is missing. Choosing love is a perpetual conscious choice. When we hand our power over to the Infinite, we are making the highest human choice: to forgo our limited vision and will in favor of a Higher Will that will inspire a new way for us to look at the situation. Even a small shift in perception is already a miracle. Make one happen now.

Why do miracles have to begin with our perception? Because usually we think of a miracle as a change in reality, but really what we need first is to change the way we see and experience the reality that is in front of us. That is why the root Torah word for miracle, *neis*, also means "to be elevated." We first have to elevate our conscious contact with our Source and shift our perception. When we do that, we will begin to experience some amazing synchronicity. Think of it as a game of hide-and-seek. Keep your eyes open and start to notice how things are coming together.

Clear cooperation: In the beginning of the creation story, it says that man is made in the image of God. Maybe that's why we all worship ourselves. In all seriousness, though, the verse is certainly not to be taken literally because God doesn't look like man. Rather, it is telling us a secret about who we are and what we are capable of. Just as God is a Creator, we, being made in the image of God, are also creators. The only questions are what and how do we create?

Remember when I said you become a spiritual antenna? Well, an antenna can both receive and broadcast messages. When you are living the three conditions, the messages you send out to the

Universe are more powerful than ever before. The thoughts you think, the words you say, and the actions you perform are all different messages you are sending out. Now that you are tuned in to that higher frequency, those messages are picked up and sent back.

When you set your intention and desire on a particular outcome, you are putting a cup in the great sea of potential and drawing some of its water into a very specific shape. You have been given the power to co-create and partner with the Infinite. Today we call it manifesting or the law of attraction, but throughout history, it has been called the power of prayer and miracles.

When you're feeling good and in alignment with the infinite power of love, you can literally change your entire life. Even if things have seemed to be going in the wrong direction for years, you can begin to turn them around in an instant. All it takes is a moment of clarity to shift your consciousness back into alignment and allow things to flow. Infinite possibilities and a world of love exist under the surface layer of reality.

We send out messages and interact with the Universe in four forms: physical, verbal, mental, and energetic. We tend to think of our power to create or accomplish anything as being limited to one, maybe two dimensions within us, so let me give you a metaphor to help you understand this idea better.

Let's say you're really excited about a new book that just came out. There are four ways you can try to get it. The first way, physical co-creation, is to get up, go to a bookstore, and purchase a copy of the book. This is the power of action, the power of your body. The second way, verbal co-creation, is to ask someone else to go get it for you. This is what we call delegating, the power of communication, and you'll achieve the same result with much less effort and energy. This is already a higher dimension of consciousness than the thought that you have to do everything yourself. The third way, mental co-creation, happens when you think of the book and your excitement about it triggers a series of synchronistic events. For instance, you may be on the way to run some errands at the drugstore, and while you're in line, you notice that they happen to be giving away free copies of the book to people who have a purchase of $20 or more, which you do. Whoa! That's magical. This is synchronicity at its best. Things like this happen all the time when you open your eyes to them. And the more you open your eyes to them, the more you'll expect them. The more you acknowledge synchronicity, the more it will show up for you.

This leads us to the fourth way, co-creation through conscious directed energy. This is the dimension in which you focus your energy in the direction of what you desire. You intentionally think, speak, and act on something you want with the intent of drawing it into your life. Unlike the drugstore, where it feels as if someone is listening to your thoughts and wants to help you out, the power of your creative thought and creative word bridges the gap between the limited and the unlimited, the manifested and the unmanifested. This is where you realize that all of nature is miraculous.

The Talmud says that the one who experiences miracles isn't aware of them. That's because those who live with miracles don't see them as miraculous anymore. They almost begin to expect them. They see miracles as a natural part of life and therefore as nature. When you realize that everything in the world is really a miracle, including your breath, the food you eat, and gravity, then you can recognize that miracles are not only possible but are happening all the time, everywhere. When you know this, it's not crazy to ask and look for what might seem miraculous to most. The One who makes oil burn can do the same with water if it is needed.

In both the third and fourth dimensions of manifesting, we are actively participating in the flow of life before taking obvious action. Your feelings are the most powerful message you broadcast. That is why you start the spiritual journey with your emotional state as well as your belief in the Infinite. Prayer has more to do with what you feel and want than what you think and say. You are literally made like a magnet. The Zohar literally explains how your emotional state directly impacts your external reality. The more joyful you are, the more revealed goodness you will experience. Everything in this world is energy, and all energy attracts like energy. It's as simple as that.

It is for this reason that the Talmud explains that the best time to pray is first thing in the morning, before you start your day. It's all about being in that purely natural state before you engage in any number of psychic poisons, such as meaningless or negative conversations, overindulgence in physical pleasures, and of course the big ones such as watching the news or checking your email, phone, and social media. These all have the capacity to immediately drag you into a more self-oriented and materialistic space or, worse, into negativity. When you are living in alignment, your thoughts start lining up with the external reality that's all around you, and life can be really fun. You will expect synchronicity and be on the lookout for signs and cues for what to do and where to go next.

The fourth dimension is where you can take all of that positive energy and connection and intend certain outcomes to start coming toward you. This is where the power of your thoughts and speech becomes apparent. The Zohar says it is through our creative word that we co-create a new earth and reality, one of positivity, love, and goodness. The power is within you.

You are now ready to infuse your thoughts and words with good feeling and faith. The first step is to clearly know and feel what you want. That could be an object, a job, a relationship, internal healing, or anything else you can dream of. In fact, this can happen even when you are standing in direct contrast to what you want because in the moment of feeling that discomfort, you will know exactly what you do want instead. Whenever you allow your mind to dwell on anything and give it your attention, you are essentially expressing your desire and will to experience it. In other words, the first stage in asking is feeling that which you desire. It is the first stage in expressing your will to receive it.

When you speak, you are concretizing and focusing your thoughts and bringing the energy of your desire from a more ethereal state of thought to a more expressed state of speech. In the same way, when you speak your thoughts, you draw the flow closer to a physical reality. This is the meaning of the proverb "Reveal your desire to God and that will create the base for the manifestation of your thoughts." You don't know how or when the flow will show up for you, but you don't have to. This is the power of surrendered manifesting. You just have to do your part. Every time you have a desire and feel strongly about something, you are asking for it to come to you. All the blessings in the world are waiting for you. Life is waiting for you to be clear about what you want and then become an open channel to receive it. If it's flowing, keep going.

In the beginning of the creation story in Genesis, humankind is called a "living soul." Now, obviously, all created beings, and certainly animals, are animated and alive. This begs the question, what is the uniqueness of humans? The accepted spiritual interpretation is that we are a spirit of speech, but this notion bothered me for nearly a decade. That isn't really all that unique, is it? Animals communicate. Today there are studies showing that plants communicate as well. Who knows, in time we might discover that seemingly inanimate objects also communicate and send energetic messages to one another. If so, why is speech so intimately associated with the essence of who we are?

Even though communication is special, your ability to communicate what you want, feel, or think isn't what makes *you* unique. Your ability to *create* reality through speech is. There is a big difference between "talk" and "speech." Spiritually speaking, when you *talk*, there is no difference between you and any other communicating being. But when you *speak*, you can change realities. Speech is your creative word. Your word is as powerful as your presence, and your presence is your essence. When you are aligned with the truth of who you are, experiencing the love of the world, and feeling good, your word becomes electrified with the power to shift reality. Rebbe Nachman of Breslov says, "Your word is as powerful as your presence."

When you speak with intention, you change the game of life. Everything you say affects the world, but what makes it magical is your consciousness. What makes it miraculous is your intention and your inner energy field. What you are feeling is your ceiling. When you are totally open to the infinite possibilities of reality, experiencing gratitude and appreciation for everything you have, and focusing on living as the best version of you rather than outcomes, your speech will direct this flow and influence everything in your reality.

Every morning, I work to align myself and focus my energy for the day. I ask myself, *What am I excited about today? What do I want to experience today?* Well, I know the answer to that. I love where I am, and I first focus on the present and all the good in my life. I then become excited about a new and potentially glorious day, about the miracles that are happening and will happen, about spiritual surprises, new insights, and successes. About the gifts of joy and peace, about knowing love even more deeply. About the opportunities to practice what I know to be true and show up to challenges better equipped than the day before. I am excited about the fun of life and the mystery to unfold.

So I ask you, what are you excited about? What do you want to experience today? First thing in the morning, no matter what happened the day before or what work lies ahead of you that day, ask yourself this question and try to listen for what awakens your inner enthusiasm. It doesn't have to be a massive change or a huge undertaking. It can be as simple as your morning coffee. Whatever it is, it has to be real, which means it has to resonate and feel right. If you could be excited about a small step forward from where you are at this moment, then that is already exciting. The Universe rewards small steps in the right direction. What does it look like, feel like, and sound like to move forward? Imagine it. Feel into it. And get excited about the journey toward whatever it is, even if it's something as small as *I'd like some relief today. I want relief.* That itself is a crystal-clear intention.

If I am looking forward to something in particular, I meditate on it and verbalize it. Prayer is simply your expressed will or desire.

That means every time you have a thought about wanting something, it is a prayer to the Universe for you to receive whatever it is. I pray for everything, and so do you, whether you realize it or not. That is why King David says, "I *am* prayer."[6] That's the essence of who we are. We are wanters, meaning we are pray-ers. The question isn't whether you pray; the question is whether you are conscious of it and deliberate about where you direct your focus.

Now, I want to give you some super practical steps on how to use your creative power to co-create the life you want to experience. First, let's break it down as simply as possible; then we can dive into a more detailed and expanded path. The steps are simple: ask, believe, then let go and receive. That's it. The Torah and every other spiritual path teach this in one version or another. I've found the easiest way to explain this process is via the message of spiritual teacher Esther Hicks.

> **Step one: Ask.** The Universe will always prompt you to question and clarify what you do and don't want. Your desire, clarity, and focus on what you do want is what you're asking for, whether that translates into verbal asking, writing it down, or simply thinking about it more often. Asking comes from a place of feeling that something is missing, isn't good enough yet, or needs a change.

> **Step two: The Universe delivers.** The Zohar teaches that from the moment the words leave your mouth in prayer, the prayer is answered on a spiritual, energetic level. It now only needs to find a way to manifest in your life. Ask and you shall receive. Ask and it is given. Step two asks you to believe in this truth.

> **Step three: Receive.** This is about tuning in to the higher frequency of who you are, that space of equanimity and joy. Remember, behind all our collective desires, we all want the same things: to feel good, to feel love, joy, and peace. We all

want to be in alignment. That is the real desire behind every yearning we have. So when you can step into this space and know you already have everything you want, you become a vessel to receive. Whereas step one is the energy of striving, step three is the energy of arriving. You step into receiving mode the moment you tap into the miracle mindset. Rav Eliyahu Dessler, a twentieth-century Torah scholar, wrote that the flow is always coming down from above, and that it is only we below who need to become receivers of that flow. This is about living in the surrendered reality that all is well, that things are working out for you, and that you will receive exactly what you need in your life and for your spiritual development at exactly the right time.

That's it. It's really that simple.

Now, if you're looking for some more guidance, here is the process that I've found to be incredibly helpful and useful over the years, a more expanded version of the three steps.

The Ten Steps of Co-creating Blessing

Step One: Ask

1. **Choose:** What is your blessing? What miracle are you excited to experience? What are you trying to co-create? Fix your mind on exactly what you're looking for. Let it be clear and specific instead of vague like "a lot of money" or "a spouse." How much money? What kind of person are they? What color hair do they have? Don't limit yourself in your thinking. The only limitations are the ones you accept. The purpose of being deliberate is that the clarity feels good. The more you can picture and clarify exactly what you're looking for, the better it will feel, and the better it feels, the more you'll tune in to the frequency of what you want. That is already priming you to receive the blessing.

2. **Set a date:** When do you believe it is possible to receive this? Whatever the answer is for you, it has to resonate and feel right. It has to be believable, not to anyone else but to you. If someone else feels that they can do it in a week but you feel that it will take a year, go with a year. Don't limit yourself in either direction based on how others might perceive the same situation. Decide ahead of time when you expect to receive your miracle. Doing this is important so that you can get a mental picture of what it will look like to receive what you are looking for. It makes it more concrete and real for you. This step is about focusing and clarifying your level of belief in the possibility of what you're moving toward.

3. **Ask:** If it's good for you, God will bend over backward to bring you your heart's desire as long as you are clear. This step not only triggers a cosmic chain of events but does so by increasing your humility as a receiver.

4. **Be willing:** Do you really want this? Decide what you are willing to do to create the space for your blessing to enter your life. It is your willingness to create the space that ultimately creates it. It isn't even your actions; they just support and reflect your willingness to connect with your desire. It is your aligned will and belief that can move mountains. You don't have to make sacrifices per se, but you do need to know how clear you are in your intention to move toward your desire. Are you willing to have fun along the way? Are you dead set on this being hard work, or are you willing to be joyful in the process? Are you willing to dedicate time and energy to this? Are you willing to be open to spiritual guidance? Are you willing to take risks and chances? Or are you willing to allow the Universe to bring things to you in its own time without requiring much from you? Whatever it is, making this clear will be a helpful guide for you.

5. **Make a plan:** You have to have a plan of action for what you are going to do to achieve your desire. It doesn't matter how small or ridiculous the plan is as long as there is something you can do to start moving in that direction. Don't wait to have the perfect plan. Just start doing something right away. What makes sense to you today might not make sense to you tomorrow, but don't wait until tomorrow. Sometimes tomorrow never comes. Be open to your plans changing, and listen for that inner guidance, those intuitive hits, impulses, and feelings. In fact, sometimes the plan will unfold as "flashes" of inspiration that feel a bit like a sixth sense. Treat them with respect and act on them when they are received. When you receive a mental download, don't ignore it. That is your Universal guidance. Listen to your intuition.

6. **Start writing:** Whenever you put pen to paper, you are signing a spiritual contract between yourself and your life Source. Write down steps one through four clearly, and read them as part of a daily or weekly ritual. The main goal is to stay in alignment with what makes you excited. Remember, it truly is about the joyful journey toward what you want. I want you to receive your dreams and miracles, but it's more important that you focus on who you are and what your life looks like as you're moving toward them. Being joyful, laughing, and having fun are the goals of reading your statement. If it gives you anxiety to keep checking it, it's not doing its job. If it brings you into the zone, helps you think clearly, and reminds you of what's possible, then it is helping you in your process.

Steps Two and Three: Believe and Receive

7. **Visualize:** Close your eyes and imagine yourself already receiving your blessing. Remember, the Zohar says the

moment you've asked, you've already been given. Step into that reality. Imagine that reality. Feel its truth and the gratitude you'd have if your blessing were here now. Hear what you'd sound like, see what you'd look like, and feel into the imagery of what you and your life will be like when you are already there. Be there fully. Sit in these sensations for a few minutes and see how you feel. The more you come back to this feeling space, the more aligned you will become with your desired outcome. This creates the space for flow.

8. **Keep it quiet:** There is no need to run around telling everyone what you are working on. Yes, there are times when it's necessary and even helpful to share your dreams with those closest to you, but as a rule, blessing falls where it is hidden from the eyes of others. The very last thing you need is the energy of somebody else who might not be as optimistic and plugged in as you interfering with your frequency. Even when people start to notice that you are excited about this, you'll have to keep perspective. Don't let anyone get you down and mentally cast a spell on your excitement. There will always be naysayers trying to stop you from pursuing your dreams or poisoning the well of your spiritual connection. Let them be them, and you be you. Drop their opinion and strengthen your own. Get excited about it, and have fun as life starts unfolding in your way. Never mind what anybody says, especially when you are in the midst of a temporary defeat. In all great success stories, the protagonist experienced these defeats before the breakthrough. Every failure brings a seed of success.

9. **Believe it:** Genuinely believing that what you desire not only is possible but will come at the right time is the energy that supercharges your will. Believing that you can

and will receive is what makes you ready to receive. Don't just say, "Well, I hope it happens." Know and believe that this will manifest in your life because you are part of the infinite love of the Universe and you are being guided toward your highest good. Be open to knowing that the reality you seek is already here, ready and waiting to be received in the perfect time.

10. **Let go and receive:** This is where you stay in alignment, surrender to life and perfect timing, and allow things to unfold exactly as they are meant to. You can't rush perfection—it's always on time. Instead of chasing your dreams, allow your dreams to chase you. Let the loving guidance of the Universe bridge the silent gap between your mind and the outer world. This also means being humbly resigned to the fact that you are not creating your blessing; rather, you are creating the space for the blessing to enter your life. It's about tuning in to that which has been created for you. If it is indeed a blessing to you, it will show up at the right time. Remember, there is a plan greater than your own, so accept that if it is not coming, it isn't yet truly good for you.

This whole thing—life, co-creation, and spiritual development—is supposed to be fun and enjoyable. There's no need to be anxious or down about it not working. It's a spiritual law of nature. It works; you work. All is well. You are always given exactly what you need for the next step in your spiritual evolution. Keep your heart open. Stay positive. Don't put any extra pressure on yourself. And know that all is well.

Cosmic Orchestration

When I was writing my last book, *It's All the Same to Me*, I had an unexplainable inner knowing that it would be a *Wall Street Journal* bestseller and that Deepak Chopra would be part of the process. I didn't understand how; it was just a strong and clear inner knowing. When I finished writing the book, I printed a mock copy of it with mock endorsements. I playfully put a quotation from Deepak on it and kept that mock book on my desk during the publishing process. I also took a screenshot of the *Wall Street Journal* bestseller page and edited it to look as if my book were the number-one bestseller in its opening week. I hung that picture up in front of my desk and periodically looked at it with this inner knowing. Even with all the work I put into writing that book, it was still a miraculous moment when that moment finally arrived. It landed at number eight on the list, and I was grateful to have reached so many people, including the kind words received from the wonderful Deepak.

One of the more powerful examples in my life was when my friend Dennis called me one day to talk about a new book project he was working on. I didn't really have the time, but something inside told me to take the call and help him with whatever he needed. I am so grateful for how people helped me in my process, so I always see it as a pleasure and a privilege to help when I can. We spoke for about an hour before he mentioned that he had a relationship with the CEO of a certain publishing house; at the time, that was exciting because I wanted to publish internationally. He offered to make an introduction, and a week later, I had a meeting set up with the CEO.

We sat down and instantly connected. A week later, I was offered a publishing deal. It was amazing. It all happened so fast. But when I started reading the fine print, it didn't actually look like a good deal. I didn't know much about the book industry at the time, but something didn't feel right. My friend Zev suggested that I reach out to some people who are heavily involved in the business side of publishing to get clarity before making any decisions. So I did just that.

I looked up literary agents and publishing houses, and I sent a number of emails, but nobody responded. I came across the Deborah Harris Agency, one of the premier agencies in Israel, and all I wanted was about ten minutes with someone who could tell me if I was being offered a good or bad deal. Rena is one of the more accessible agents at Deborah Harris, so I sent her a message. About a week later, she responded that she'd be happy to engage in a conversation and help me out. I was so grateful.

"I don't think it's a good deal; you probably shouldn't sign it. Second of all, I think that if you're a writer and you've had so much success already, you should consider getting an agent so you could really reach more people," Rena said.

"Well, how do I do that?" I asked.

She explained the process, then said she'd be happy to take a look at my book and give it to one of her friends who was in the nonfiction world, as she only worked with fiction. I thanked her for her time, sent her the manuscript, thought nothing more of it, and went on with my day. A week later, she sent me an email saying she wanted to call and talk about the manuscript.

When we got on the phone, she said, "Look, I have to tell you even though I don't read self-help or nonfiction, I fell in love with your manuscript. It spoke to me on many levels, and even though I don't represent nonfiction, nor do I even read it, I would like to represent your book if you'd give me the chance." *What? How did this happen? Did I just get an offer from an agency?* "I love that you are bringing Torah to the world stage, and I'd like to be a part of that," she continued. I was taken aback as well as grateful, happy, and excited.

An agent had seemingly shown up right in front of me, wanting to be part of the dream of sharing this wisdom. Thanks to the call with Dennis that I almost hadn't taken, I received a publishing deal and found my agent, Rena, and Deborah Harris. Several months later, we started working on the proposal for my new book. We'd heard back from some of my favorite publishing houses, but one message sounded special, from Diana Ventimiglia at Sounds True. She wanted to hop on a call with me, and Rena said that was a good sign.

Rena, Diana, and I met in a Zoom call, and Diana asked some basic questions about me, my book, and what inspired me to write it.

Then she started pitching us on why we should consider signing with Sounds True. She seemed excited about the book and all that could be possible if we worked together. I can't imagine that all publisher calls are conducted like that.

And then she said it: "I have to tell you, I was kind of geeking out when I found out we were going to be on a call together. I've been so excited." Now I was really confused. "I read your other book." I scratched my head, knowing we hadn't sent her the first book. "You see, about a year ago, my mother passed away during the height of the pandemic. I was struggling and feeling a lot of grief. My friend Tova handed me a book and said, 'I think this might help you.' It was called *It's All the Same to Me*. It was one of the few things that gave me relief during that time. It was and still is an important book in my life, and I was waiting to see your next book, not as a publisher but as a reader. When I opened up my inbox and saw the email from Rena about me being the potential editor for your next book, I was so excited and couldn't believe it!"

My jaw dropped. I could not believe what I was hearing. It was as if God, in eternal knowing, had set things in motion a year prior for the perfect arrival of divine timing on all fronts. We signed with Sounds True, and I love working with Diana. This whole experience has been a blessing in its own right. This is synchronicity, this is manifestation, this is a modern-day miracle.

What If It's Not Working?

People often say to me, "I have prayed for things in the past, and it didn't work. How do I look at my ability to create if it's just not happening for me? I have done the whole manifesting thing, and it's really hit or miss." To this, I say the following. Whether you call it manifesting, prayer, setting intentions, or meditating, the ultimate goal is your alignment and spiritual evolution. It's all about awakening. It's all about your presence. We always have to turn back to our life's purpose when we co-create. We are here to actualize our unique potential and develop our awareness of spirit.

When we authentically pray or meditate, we are elevating ourselves in the process. Whether or not we get what we are looking for in the physical world is less important than the connection we make with the love of the Universe during the journey. You can rise above fear and ego, embrace the love of your soul and the love of your life, and step into the light of peace and joy. Yes, you have certain desires for your life, and you always will, but the inner truth of what you are living for comes through every time you step into surrendered manifesting.

The humility of seeing yourself as a co-creator and a space creator rather than *the* Creator will serve your expansion, and the essence of what we all desire and crave in this life will ultimately be fulfilled. Knowing that you are essentially a receiver that helped direct the flow is what brings blessings down to you. Let go and let yourself be guided. Live in trust and create a channel for flow to enter your life right now. The unfortunate catch twenty-two is that standing in resistance to what's happening in your life and feeling anxious or upset about it is ultimately what continues the block. Fear, doubt, and all the lower-level frequencies keep us out of tune with what we truly desire, both in the world of spirit and in the world of form.

When you feel this way, don't underestimate the power of hope. Sure, there is a powerful psychological component of hope that we can all recognize, but spiritually, hope is a catalyst for miracles. Hope isn't to be taken lightly, and it isn't flimsy. It is a deep knowing that there are infinite possibilities. Hope in this context is synonymous with faith, belief, and trust. When you trust in love and earnestly look to God with hope for a resolution to any situation, you've created a cosmic change.

This is where surrender comes in. It's not about giving up; it's about giving over control. No outcomes are yours, and all outcomes are good. Sometimes the blessing is waiting for you to plug in to alignment, and with your intention, will, or prayer, you actually have the power to draw that flow into your life. At other times, however, for whatever higher reason there is, what you desire isn't the highest good, and the situation won't change. When we pray for guidance and set our intentions, we simultaneously have to hold the space of knowing that all outcomes are for our highest good. "Surrendered manifesting" is the truth behind any and all ideas we have about our ability to create with our minds. We are only ever space creators, receivers, and directors of energy. We don't create the energy itself. Ultimately, all creativity and flow happen from a deeper dimension of reality. Nothing new is ever born without the willingness of the highest love and intention we can perceive. However, we have the incredible ability to create the space for blessing to come into our lives and the lives of others.

This may be one of the most fundamental points in this book. While it is indeed true that you can use your God-given gifts to achieve and receive your heart's desire, it isn't true that you can do and have *whatever* you want here-now. Behind all of our individual wills is a Superwill, the Ultimate Desire of Life, which is the innermost point of love in the world. It's what we call God or Source, and, in truth, it is the source of our inner being. This is what guides and assists every being in experiencing their purpose. We will discuss this more at length in the final chapter, but for right now, what's important is recognizing that we don't create; we reveal what already exists. In other words, we create the space for flow to come in or not, and that depends on a will greater than our own.

This is one of the beautiful reasons behind the idea of Shabbat, or the Sabbath. Every weekend, I spend close to twenty-six hours totally disconnected from the internet, my phone, and any work-related activities, including conversations about them. It is a time to completely disconnect and return to the source of all my energy. During that time, I let go, surrender, and remember that the true flow of all creativity doesn't come from me; rather it comes from something much deeper. It is a truly liberating and soulful time.

You can do everything when you realize you're not the One doing anything. Everything is already there and ready for you. Your job is to tune in and draw from that pool of infinite potential in your life.

King Solomon says, "Trust in God with all of your heart and don't rely on your own understanding."[7] He is saying to trust in the light of love and don't ever think you have all the answers. Of course we're supposed to move toward whatever end we're aiming for, but on the inside we have to leave room for something bigger and more creative to enter our lives. When we can let go of the outcome, we can have fun and enjoy the process, stay in alignment and in the present moment, and joyfully anticipate what will happen next. In this space, synchronicities abound. The world is working out for us. Even though we're often waiting to see miracles, usually the miracles are waiting for us to see them.

Give no resistance to life, and it will flow in a magical way. It's all about learning how to swim in your stream. Be open to the fact that you don't know what the best outcome is, and trust that you are being guided to something amazing. This isn't being passive; it is actively leaning in and trying to learn from the greatest teacher: life.

In the next chapter, we'll bring everything together and discuss what your life can look and feel like when your newfound power is charged with your purpose. The difference between a meaningful life and a meaningless one has less to do with what you are able to create or accomplish than with why you do so.

CHAPTER EIGHT

Living a Meaningful Life

It's time to ask yourself, *What kind of reality do I really want to create, and why?* As I mentioned earlier, everyone has an inner and outer purpose to their life. Only you can determine your outer purpose—your personal life, your career, the relationships you engage in, the material things you purchase, where you live, and all things that are external to the essence of who you are. That is the fun part of your journey that nobody gets to limit and decide for you. Of course you will want to go out and be productive, achieve, and live as the best version of who you can be, but that is only half of what you are doing here in this world. You can focus your energy on the outer, material reality, and that's an essential part of what you're doing here. If God wanted us all to be solely spiritual beings and glowing energies, we wouldn't have physical bodies in a physical world with physical desires. In addition to all of this is knowing that you're here for something much bigger. You have purpose. You're part of the collective, and we are all in this together.

We have always been on a journey of spiritual evolution, but now more than ever a global awakening of consciousness is taking place, and the fact that you are reading this right now means that, on some level, you are ready and on the frontier. Listen to what reverberates inside you. Listen to what resonates, that inner voice that softly calls you in its direction.

Now is the time. This is the place. You are the one.

The inner part of purpose is the same for all of us. We are here to experience and express True Love. In the language of scripture, we are here to know God and share that with the world around us, to know our soul for what it truly is: a spark of the divine. You have to know who you are, what you're doing here, and how you're doing it. You are the light bringing the light by being the light. Make this your life's mantra: "I am the light bringing the light by being the light." Life is simple. There's no need to overcomplicate things. I believe the Talmud sums up the message of life perfectly: we are here to shine like the sun. We all know people who shine. They seem to have a different energy and tone of voice, and they brighten any room they enter. There are three traits that will be ascribed to you when you shine and live with love.

First, when being insulted, don't insult back. It doesn't mean you just hold your tongue when you're insulted or shamed. It means you don't internally lash out at those who speak negatively to or about you. You're nonresistant. Imagine if you were transparent, and others' words just went through you. What others say to you would become irrelevant. When you just don't care anymore about the opinions of others, you live a different life. You start to shine. It doesn't matter what people say or think about you if you know that what you are doing is right and moral. Be at peace with who you are, and you will shine.

Second, your actions are from and for love. There are only ever two reasons for acting: because you have to or because you want to. In other words, you act only out of fear or from love. The more you live your life with passion and love for what you are doing, the more you'll shine. If you feel that everything in your life is a chore and that you *have* to do something because otherwise everything falls apart, you cover up the light of your soul. You shine when you are in love with life, and you find love when you find meaning. When what you are doing is meaningful and purposeful to you, you can be in love with both menial tasks and daunting deadlines. When you realize that there are good and love in all situations, you can be in love all the time. Act from love and for love, and you will shine.

Third, you'll be able to stay happy and positive even in the face of challenges. Of course it's easy to be happy when everything is going well, but how do you respond when things become challenging? As we discussed in the chapter on certainty, this is all about leaning into love and a bigger picture of what your life is about. When you befriend the present moment, accepting it as it is and surrendering to it fully, you know that every situation is happening *for* you and not *to* you; you live with grace. Living in gratitude is the key step. You will know that every mistake you make is there for you to learn a valuable lesson or to get you somewhere you need to be.

The Torah word for challenges is *yesurin*, which means "to remove." Every challenge has the potential to remove a layer of fakeness and help you become more real. Lean into your challenges with joy because no matter what it looks like on the outside, you are being guided in the direction of your highest good on the inside. When you see people who stand up in the face of danger or prejudice with a smile on their face, you know you are looking at someone special. When people face tragedy with faith, they shine brighter than the sun. When you can smile at your challenges, you will shine too.

One of my favorite Torah scholars, Yehuda Loew, also known as the Maharal of Prague, describes the common denominator of all three of these traits as a state of spiritual connection, a state of non-resistance, a state of love. He explains that each one reflects a person who is identified not with the outer world of form but with the inner spirit, with the inner love of reality, and with a deeper knowing of what life is about. In this, they are simple. Love is simple. This is why when things get complicated, you can be sure you are distant from the inner light. In Kaballa, every Hebrew letter also represents a number. The Hebrew word for *love* shares the same numerical value as the word for *one*. When you find yourself in love, you find yourself at one with whatever it is you are loving. There is nothing more powerful than to be at one with all life. Loving what is.

You can love another even if they insult you, act from love even when you're most afraid, and still be in love with the Universe when tests are sent your way. You can do this when you are at one with what is. When you live in the now, in the present, and yield to the journey of life instead of trying to steer the river, you will shine your light on life. People will have no choice but to notice. Your energy will uplift a room.

There are sparks of love in every person you meet, every situation you experience, and every place you go. We have been gifted with the ability to elevate and reveal the goodness and help the world come back together. Don't just feel love—be love. Don't just look for pleasure—look for ways to share it with others. Kindness, justice, and truth—these are the gifts that keep giving.

Nevertheless, here is the problem, if there is any, with the world: we are not collectively in touch with the soul of our planet. From the outside in, the world is broken and needs fixing. The world is sick and needs healing. The world is out of balance and needs harmony. The world is lacking and needs fulfillment. The world is suffering and needs peace. The world is sad and needs joy. The world is dark and needs light. The world has a question, and you, my friend, are the answer.

Be the fixing, be the healing, be the harmony, be the fulfillment, be the peace and the joy. Be the light and shine like the sun. Be an instrument of love in the world. Return to love and appreciation. With every prayer you say, every kind word you speak and action you do, and every positive thought you have, you are changing the energy of the world. You are elevating and glorifying the presence of love in life. In Chasidus, this is referred to as bringing the Shechina out of Galus, or bringing the indwelling, loving presence of God out of exile—the loving presence of God that has been lost in the world. You make a difference today and every day. You are here to help bring the world one step closer to alignment. You are powerful, and you are the only one who can do your part in this. My closest mentor, Rabbi Beryl Gershenfeld, always reminds me that we are more rarefied than any precious stone. You are one of a kind. Literally once in a universal history. Nobody else can do what you are here to do.

You can embody this knowing when you live a life that is filled with miracles and joy. We are not only meant to *feel* happy, peaceful, and loving; it is what we're doing here. We're not just supposed to experience miracles. No, that is our mission. We are all miracle workers and light workers, and if this fact resonates with you, take it as confirmation that, without a doubt, that is what you're here to do. Look deeply within yourself and identify your unique gifts. What circumstances were you given, and where were you placed? Where are you in history, and who is your social network? Once you are in love with your life, notice that everything you have been given is an opportunity for you to express your creative love in this life.

What is the highest human achievement? True humility. You see, there is an inner struggle between our ego and our inner knowing that we are all great. In fact, we're so great that we're made in the image of God, yet at the same time, we know we're as fleeting as dust in the wind. What usually happens is that we choose one side and go with it. We feel either proud and strong or weak and ashamed. Both of these are ego manifestations. The part of you that judges others and the part of you that plays the victim are both wrong. The truth of humility is realizing our sameness. To the ego, I always want to be first. To the soul, I know that there is no second. This is the key. On the outside, we all play different roles, but on the deepest level, we are all the same. You don't have more or less power than the person sitting next to you. We are all space creators. Whether something comes into that space has nothing to do with you. This is the greatest power you have: to know the truth of who you are and partner with the loving presence of the Universe to co-create a better reality than what exists at this moment.

Your body can be as aggressive as a wolf and your soul as gentle as a sheep. There is a verse in Isaiah that says we have collectively arrived at spiritual awakening when "the wolf will dwell with the sheep . . . for the world will be filled with the knowing of God."[1] There is a purpose to all of this: to know God. To know love. To know your very essence and the essence of all things, the life force of the world. To know the Godliness within every person you meet, every situation you experience, and everything you come in contact with. To know is to feel is to shine. You'll take inspired action when you're in alignment. This is the future. We are all part of the ongoing revelation of divine consciousness in the world. Our life is a passageway from God with God for God to God. Or from Love with Love for Love to Love. There are two ways to be a part of the unfolding of Consciousness: to know that you already are and to not know. All you have is your awareness; that is who you are. You can be it fully. You can be it now.

Make the decision today to make peace in your relationships that need it most. If that's not possible, make peace with them in your mind. You don't need another human being to heal. It starts with you. Take one thing in your life that you give yourself a hard time about and forgive yourself today. Don't let another day go by with any self-deprecation. You deserve better. Forgive the people who have hurt you, and release them from being the weight that is slowing you down and holding you back from the life you deserve. You don't need to forgive others because they deserve it. Forgive them because you love yourself enough to stop the pain. The golden rule is to love others as you love yourself. Well, first you have to love yourself, whether that means breaking up with the person who is ruining your life or marrying the person who actually makes you happy. Breathe deeply today, and enjoy the ride of your life.

The battle of human reality is between negative and positive beliefs. We are allowed negative thoughts so that we can work to overcome them with positivity, love, and goodness. This is the essential purpose of your life. This is what creates your ability to return to your Godly essence. We change our life when we change our beliefs about life.

Look at the world today. It is amazing how far we have come. In all fields, we have advanced beyond the wildest dreams of our ancestors. It is a gift to be alive today and see all that is happening and know that we are at the tip of the iceberg. So much more is to come and unfold, and we get to be here to witness a great part of it. Today there are more freedoms and liberties than ever before; there is better medicine and health, more equality and peace, better technology and science, and more global connection. Nevertheless, we still have a lot of work to do. You may not be able to affect climate change, politics, Hollywood, or international wars with your smile today, but I guarantee that your smile affects how things will unfold tomorrow. The Universe has been moving in this direction for as long as it's been around, and we are very close to experiencing the Garden of Eden right here on earth.

The Torah begins with the letter *Bet*, which has the numerical value of two. Its significance is that the world was created when duality and separation were created. The rest of history is a backward-moving process, from two back to one, from separation to unity, from fear to love. Imagine just for a moment that the energy of the world is made out of letters, and the things we see and experience are the words. With that in mind, the world is telling a story. It is the greatest drama, romance, thriller, and comedy ever to be written. We have become so consumed by the story that we have forgotten what it is actually about. The story of life is the story of God, the story of the light emerging from the darkness. It is the story of our souls bringing harmony back to the world when we start reading the story the right way again.

There is a well-known ancient metaphor about a hunter who goes to Africa. There, he finds a tree with a number of beautiful parrots perching on the branches. He thinks, *What a beautiful breed of parrots. I will take one home with me.* After setting a trap, he successfully retrieves his parrot and heads back to his native home. After a number of months, the hunter and the parrot become the best of friends, and he sincerely takes great care of it.

Years later, the hunter decides to return to that same area. He turns to the parrot and asks, "Is there anything you want me to tell the other parrots for you?"

"Yes," the parrot responds. "Please tell them that I am happy and well taken care of in my cage. Life is good here."

The hunter goes on his way, and when he arrives, he once again finds the tree with the beautiful birds. Raising his voice, he yells the message of his beloved parrot up into the tree. Then, the strangest thing happens. One of the parrots falls right out of the tree, dead on the spot. The man thinks how strange this is but continues on his way. When he returns home, the parrot asks him if he delivered the message.

"Yes. I told them, but then something weird happened. Upon hearing your message, one of the parrots died and fell out of the tree."

Upon hearing this, the parrot in the cage falls over and dies. Totally confused and a little shaken, he takes his parrot out to the porch and places it on a pile of wood. A moment later, his beloved parrot jumps up and dusts itself off.

"Hey, you tricked me! Why did you do that?" the hunter says.

The parrot looks at the hunter and says, "My brother was sending me a message. If you want to get out of your cage, you have to die now."

All the external parts of your life are like a dream. The Talmud says if you really want to live, then die before you die. Let go of the shell you're in while you're alive so you can get out of the cage that holds you. Then, share the message with everybody else.

Not long before I made the decision to leave the rock band, I invited a friend over for Friday-night dinner. We called it for 7 pm, but as I continually glanced at the clock, it quickly went from 7:15 to 7:45. I looked at the food on the counter and realized that he wasn't going to show up. My table faced the door, and I had left it wide open so I could hear him if he was lost and looking for my place, but what happened instead changed my life. My neighbor Alex, whom I had been cordial with but never really spoken to, saw me sitting there waiting and said, "Hey, come on over and join us."

Alex, his partner, their roommate, and I sat around the dinner table for about an hour and a half, talking about the band, touring, and all the great things we had accomplished.

Then, Alex looked at me and said, "Moshe, it looks like you have something weighing on you. What's on your mind?"

I realized then that he had a keen sense of people because we had just met, and there he was, absolutely right. I told him I was having second thoughts about the band.

"Well, do you have a picture of what you would like your life to look like in ten years?"

I hadn't thought about it until he asked me, but I closed my eyes and saw a vision of who I wanted to be. It was so clear. I started describing the vision of a young man who was married with children, walking his kids to school, being involved in community work, and helping and assisting others with their spiritual pursuits. When I finished describing the vision I had seen, I looked at Alex, and his eyes were filled with tears.

"Alex, I know I paint a pretty picture, but why on earth are you so emotional about it?"

He looked me in the eyes and said, "I had that kind of clarity once. I chose to listen to others about what I should do and how I should live my life. I didn't want to go to law school, but I did because of my parents, my scholarship, and a lot of external pressure. It's been ten years, and I am just figuring that out now. Every day that goes by that you don't take a step in the direction of your vision, you are adding a black-and-white pixel onto the screen of your life. Soon, the vision will be gone, the inspiration will fade, and you will have had your life chosen for you instead of choosing your life for yourself. Make a decision and start today."

After he said those words, I was changed. It was a moment of grace, a moment where I was given another chance and an opportunity to start again and live a life I wanted to live. They say people who are successful make decisions quickly and change their minds slowly. People who aren't successful make decisions slowly and change their minds quickly. If you know, then you know. You can take a step or an entire leap. It's up to you.

My gift to you in this book is an opportunity to make a change today and not care about the conditions of others but rather the three conditions of your soul. These are the conditions that make you human, keep you alive, and open you up to a world of infinite possibilities, and the fulfillment of knowing what you are here to do and be. I wish you much blessing, success, love, and guidance in everything you will experience. Shine like the sun and be a light for everyone in your life. Only you have the power to create the better you. Use your gifts and live your most joyous life. Don't wait until tomorrow. Do something today to show your commitment to living that life you once considered a myth. If you're happy, you're helping. Let intention, joy, and certainty lead you to living a miraculous life. I love you.

Life: There is one. There is soul. Then there is birth and ego. There is not knowing, and there is fear. There is judgment. There is your nature, your nurture, and your societal upbringing. There is domestication and forgetting. There is pain and trouble. There is breakdown, and there is breakthrough. There is love. There is joy and fun. There is spiritual reconnection and knowing. There are miracles. There is You.

A Poem of Love

Peace is found in knowing the love of God within.

There is only separation on the outside; on
the inside is only love and peace.

There is a Soul of the world, the Good
within, and Love is within the Good.

All of its pathways lead to peace.

I can praise and thank God when things look
good, and I can do the same when they don't.

There is no place where God is not.

There is no place where Good is not.

There is no place where Love is not.

There is no place where Direction and Guidance are not.

You are a life force, the energy within all things.

Peace is what happens when you drop
the outer shell and go within.

In the Good days, be fully in the Good. In the bad days, see.

To conquer your ego is to let go of negative thinking
and fully embrace positive, loving thoughts. It takes
great strength, and through it, you become an angel.

When you let go of the negative, the shell falls away. Not
only do you see the light that was there before, but even
more light enters through the window you've created.

Stop looking at the effect and focus on the Cause.

Transform and go above physical form, beyond limitation.

God gives wisdom to the wise. When you start the process
of looking for the soul of the world, the hidden wisdom and
messages, you create a channel to receive divine insight and clarity.

Go create, and you will be created.

You were created to Know.

That is, you were created to know Unity, to know
Good, to know thy Self, to know Love.

There are two types of love: apparent, which is conditional,
and essential, which is unconditional. When you experience
the essential love of God, the unity and connection within all
things, bridging oneself with the Shechina, you experience
the unconditional love of being the emanation of God. This
is the love of redemption, the love that comes with the
deepest peace. This is the hidden light, the first creation. "The
wolf will dwell with the sheep . . . for the world is filled
with God, the world is filled with Knowing Love."

This is the future. This is the evolution of our world's
Consciousness. "There will be a day of One, known
as the day of God. A day which is not day nor night,"
above time and space, a day of peace and miracles.

The enlightened see the world with eyes of love and light right
now, today. It is from them that we draw out and learn to live
this life. "For the lips of the loving servant hold the loving
intention of God; go and receive Torah from his mouth." He
is like an angel, stripped from the negative limiting beliefs
based in fear. He has transformed and elevated. Go to Him.

If you choose to love life, love will fill it, and
you will see the hidden good.

If you want to truly live, love your days and look for the good.

Appendix

The Four Questions Tool

I want to give you a life-changing simple formula for happiness. The following four questions are the most important questions you will ever ask yourself. Each one is scored on a scale of zero to ten with a possible total score of forty. This score will reveal (1) your overall level of well-being and the general state of joy you live with and (2) the exact areas you can focus on to elevate your state of consciousness.

Once you've done your personal self-assessment, take a look at where you're ranked highest and lowest. In the areas where you rank high, lean in. You're already strong in these areas, and therefore you can likely easily strengthen your connection. In the areas where you score low, you now have an idea of what you need to develop if you are committed to living with more love, joy, and peace.

To authentically gauge yourself and get results that can help you, it's important to be as honest and authentic as possible. There's a difference between what you want to believe and what you actually believe, and you can sense that difference in how you generally feel. With this in mind, ask yourself the following four questions and answer on a scale of zero to ten, zero being No/Never and ten being Absolutely/Always.

To clarify, zero means no and never, so, for example, if you sometimes feel that things in life, including yourself, are OK, then don't answer that question with zero. In the same vein, scoring a ten is just as rare. If you give yourself a score of ten when it comes to how you feel about yourself, that would mean you never take what anybody has ever said to or about you seriously, you are never insulted, and you absolutely do not care about the opinions of others.

Last point: there are no wrong answers. This is a general test for you to see where you *feel* you are in relation to these four questions. They don't make you a better or worse person; rather they assess your overall well-being and give reflection and direction for what you can focus on to increase your levels of love, joy, and peace.

1. **Do you believe and feel that you are good (regardless of how well you perform, the mistakes you've made in the past, or the judgments of others)?**

    Zero means "I *never* feel I am inherently good, or I don't feel I am good *at all*. I completely care about what people think about me and derive my self-worth from my performance. I am a perfectionist, and my job title and possessions make me feel important. Without them, I feel like a failure."

    On the other hand, ten means "I *always* feel I am, deep down, inherently, 100 percent good, no matter what happens or what I do. I am confident, I love myself, I am always authentic no matter who I am with or what I am doing, and I have fun with my life."

    Sit for a moment and feel into this. It's not something to think about. Instead, listen to how deeply it resonates or does not, and whatever number feels right is the number you should go with. On a scale of zero to ten, do you feel that your essence is truly good, valuable, and perfect just as you are?

2. **Do you believe and feel that you have the potential and power to accomplish your dreams, goals, and desires?**

    Zero means "*Not at all*. I have *zero* ability to make my dreams a reality in my years on the planet," whereas ten means "I am 100 percent confident in my personal power to create my own reality."

    Sit for a moment and feel into this. It's not something to think about. Instead, listen to how deeply it resonates or does not, and whatever number feels right is the number you should go with. On a scale of zero to ten, do you feel that you have the ability to create your own reality?

3. **Do you believe and feel that the world is essentially good? Regardless of what goes on or has gone on, do you feel that, at its core, the Universe is good?**

    Zero means you generally feel that the world is terrible and is out to get you. You feel that the Universe is inherently problematic, chaotic, and in disorder. A ten means you generally feel that the Universe is inherently good, divine, loving, meaningful, intentional, and by design. You feel that everything, even things that appear and are experienced as "bad," has a purpose and therefore is ultimately good.

    Sit for a moment and feel into this. It's not something to think about. Instead, listen to how deeply it resonates or does not, and whatever number feels right is the number you should go with. On a scale of zero to ten, do you feel that the world is essentially good?

4. **Do you believe and feel that the Universe is supportive of you and your desires?**

    Zero means a strong "No, I'm totally on my own in the Universe, and it isn't going to help me one bit!" A ten feels more like a deep and sincere belief that an inherently good or divine Universe is fully here to support you, your soul, your purpose in being born, and all the talents, skills, and resources you have been given in this life.

    Sit for a moment and feel into this. It's not something to think about. Instead, listen to how deeply it resonates or does not, and whatever number feels right is the number you should go with. On a scale of zero to ten, do you feel that the Universe is supportive of you and your desires?

After asking yourself these questions, tally your total score and take a look at where you fall on the sliding forty-point scale. If your score is under twenty points, I can almost guarantee that you are going through life in pain. You don't have to live the rest of your life this way. You can take action today, if you're so inspired, and take steps toward a more joyous and loving life. The closer you are to forty points, the closer you are to enlightenment and pure bliss.

To put things in context, if you score between a twenty-three and a twenty-six, you likely feel that "I'm happy enough, enough of the time. Life could be better, but I'll deal with what I've got."

If you scored a thirty or above, you're likely one of the happier people in your social network. You feel that life is really great and there is much to experience, see, feel, and do. That is a relatively high total score. If you scored a thirty-three or higher, you are likely a beacon of light and/or a teacher to everyone you come in contact with.

If you'd like to get the most out of this amazing tool, I suggest that you choose a day and time once a week each month—for example, Sundays at 9:00 am—to commit to sitting down and doing this exercise. It takes all of five focused minutes. See how you assess your total scores and how much they might waver depending on what is happening in your life at the time. At the end of the month, take a look at the average total score and see where you stand.

The most important part of the tool isn't your score but what you can do about the areas that need improvement. Did you score a seven and eight about yourself but a five and six about the Universe? Did you score eights about the world and fours about yourself? Just by paying attention to what scored lower, you know exactly what needs improving, and that, my friend, is incredibly empowering. Self-awareness is key.

If you increase your positive feelings toward these questions, you will feel happier, whether it's a little or a lot. I sincerely wish you only love and blessings in your journey.

There are only two things that matter in your life.

*What you believe about your Self and what
you believe about the Universe.*

*Every single thing you do and experience in your life is
a direct expression of your paradigm in these two areas.
Therefore, absolutely nothing should be more important than
the refinement and clarity of these inner agreements.*

You get to choose what you believe.

How are you going to live?

*This is a guide to enhance your level of spiritual
empowerment and spiritual enlightenment.*

The beginning of the rest of your life starts now.

Notes

Introduction

1. Caroline Myss, *Anatomy of the Spirit: The Seven Stages of Power and Healing* (New York: Penguin Random House, 1996), 43.
2. Myss, *Anatomy of the Spirit*, 43.
3. Isaiah 11:6.

Chapter One: Wherever You Think, You Are

1. Baal Shem Tov Al HaTorah (Amud HaTefila); Tzavat HaRivash, Keser Shem Tov 2:12.
2. Proverbs 23:7.
3. Napoleon Hill, *Think and Grow Rich* (New York: Penguin Publishing Group, 2005).
4. Psalm 97:5.
5. Rebbe Nachman of Breslov, "Machshava," *Lekutai Eitzos*.
6. Psalm 126:1.

Chapter Two: The Condition of Intention

1. Ecclesiastes 7:29.
2. Deuteronomy 30:19.
3. Rav Dov Ber ben Avraham of Mezritch, also known as the Maggid of Mezritch, *Dibros Hamagid* (Atara LaRosh Tzadik Publishing, 2019), 377.
4. *Ethics of the Fathers* 1:3.

Chapter Three: Intention Applied—
Bringing Intention to Life

1. David D. Burns, *Feeling Good: The New Mood Therapy* (New York: HarperCollins Publishers, 1999), ch. 3.
2. Genesis 12:1.
3. Proverbs 14:2; Rav Shlomo Wolbe, Emunaso Yichyeh, Bais HaMusar 5773, 142.

Chapter Four: The Condition of Certainty

1. Proverbs 27:19.

Chapter Five: Applying Certainty—Living
with Love Is an Active Choice

1. Deuteronomy 5:5.
2. Deuteronomy 30:19.
3. Deuteronomy 4:4.
4. Max Planck, Nobel Peace Prize acceptance speech, June 1, 1920.
5. Helen Schucman, *A Course in Miracles* (New York: Penguin Books, 1999), 77.
6. Psalm 92:1.
7. Rabbi Joseph Karo, *The Shulchan Aruch* (1565) 1:1.
8. Ecclesiastes 7:14.

Chapter Six: The Condition of Joy

1. Don Miguel Ruiz, *The Four Agreements: A Practical Guide to Personal Freedom* (San Rafael, CA: Amber-Allen Publishing, 1997), 52.
2. Dr. Richard Carlson, *You Can Be Happy No Matter What: Five Principles for Keeping Life in Perspective* (Novato, CA: New World Library, 2006), 2.
3. Isaiah 55:12.
4. Ecclesiastes 1:2.

Chapter Seven: Synchronicity, Miracles, and Manifesting

1. Psalm 32:10.
2. Ecclesiastes 7:20.
3. Neale Donald Walsch, *Conversations with God, Book 4: Awaken the Species* (London: Watkins Media Ltd., 2018), 230.
4. Psalm 118:20.
5. Psalm 100:4.
6. Psalm 109:4.
7. Proverbs 3:5.

Chapter Eight: Living a Meaningful Life

1. Isaiah 11:6.

Additional Verses

Talmud Brachos 61a

Talmud Shabbat 31a

Talmud Shabbat 88b

Talmud Rosh Hashana 11a

Talmud Sotah 3a

Talmud Tamid 32a

Talmud Derech Eretz

Talmud Nidda 31a

Zohar Titzaveh 184b

Zohar Lech Lecha 90a

Zohar Balak 185a

Zohar Vayetzei 99b

Tikunai Zohar 105b

Acknowledgments

This book has been a real labor of love, and there are a number of people without whom it wouldn't have been possible. To the whole Sounds True team, you've been a blessing to work with. Thank you to my editors, Lyric Dodson and Diana Ventimiglia, for making this experience so enjoyable and bringing this work to life. Thank you for resonating with me and my work and shining your light upon it. My agent, Rena Rossner, and the whole Deborah Harris Agency—your belief in me and my vision, coupled with your drive to make this project come alive, is deeply appreciated. Thank you, Aba, Ema, Meir, Alex, Ma, Ta, Annette, and my entire crazy Kalfa family. Your love and support are immeasurable. Rav Beryl Gershenfeld, Rav Noach Orlowek, and Rav Asher Weiss, thank you for your instrumental support every step of the way. I am so grateful to my kids, Chaviva, Ahava, Akiva, and Aliza, for letting me have so much Aba time to work on this project. I love you with all my heart. My wife, Avigial, thank you for being my anchor in this life, keeping me focused, and being my best friend. Thank you for reviewing the manuscript countless times and sharing your priceless advice with me. None of this would be possible without you. And of course, I am grateful to God and the loving guidance You've given me every step of the way. Words will never do You justice, so I wink at You with a knowing smile and say, *Thank You.*

About the Author

Following fifteen years of in-depth comprehensive Torah study, today, Moshe Gersht is a spiritual teacher, *Wall Street Journal* and *USA Today* bestselling author, and TEDx speaker. But previously, Moshe had quite a different life, spending nearly a decade touring the United States as the singer and songwriter for a popular Los Angeles-based rock band.

With the desire to assist in the evolution of consciousness and the global awakening of humanity, he has since devoted his life to seamlessly connecting the worlds of Torah and mystical wisdom with the true nature of the human mind and our collective struggles. In addition to years of study under the guidance of the world's premier rabbis and wisdom teachers, he has found a niche sharing his love for life, people, and spirit through speaking, teaching, and writing.

About Sounds True

Sounds True was founded in 1985 by Tami Simon with a clear mission: to disseminate spiritual wisdom. Since starting out as a project with one woman and her tape recorder, we have grown into a multimedia publishing company with a catalog of more than 3,000 titles by some of the leading teachers and visionaries of our time, and an ever-expanding family of beloved customers from across the world.

In more than three decades of evolution, Sounds True has maintained our focus on our overriding purpose and mission: to wake up the world. We offer books, audio programs, online learning experiences, and in-person events to support your personal growth and awakening, and to unlock our greatest human capacities to love and serve.

At SoundsTrue.com you'll find a wealth of resources to enrich your journey, including our weekly *Insights at the Edge* podcast, free downloads, and information about our nonprofit Sounds True Foundation, where we strive to remove financial barriers to the materials we publish through scholarships and donations worldwide.

To learn more, please visit SoundsTrue.com/freegifts or call us toll-free at 800.333.9185.

Together, we can wake up the world.